I0190332

Methodism And The

Second Blessing

by

Rev. J. C. Street

First Fruits Press
Wilmore, Kentucky
c2015

Methodism and the Second Blessing, by J.C. Street.

First Fruits Press, ©2015
Previously published: Louisville, Ky. : Pentecostal Publishing Company,
[1903].

ISBN: 9781621712466 (print), 9781621712473 (digital), 9781621712480
(kindle)

Digital version at http://place.asburyseminary.edu/firstfruitsheritagematerial/104/

First Fruits Press is a digital imprint of the Asbury Theological Seminary, B.L.
Fisher Library. Asbury Theological Seminary is the legal owner of the material
previously published by the Pentecostal Publishing Co. and reserves the right to
release new editions of this material as well as new material produced by
Asbury Theological Seminary. Its publications are available for noncommercial
and educational uses, such as research, teaching and private study. First Fruits
Press has licensed the digital version of this work under the Creative Commons
Attribution Noncommercial 3.0 United States License. To view a copy of this
license, visit http://creativecommons.org/licenses/by-nc/3.0/us/.

For all other uses, contact:

First Fruits Press
B.L. Fisher Library
Asbury Theological Seminary
204 N. Lexington Ave.
Wilmore, KY 40390
http://place.asburyseminary.edu/firstfruits

Street, J. C. (James C.)
    Methodism and the second blessing / by J.C. Street.
    125 pages ; 21 cm.
    Wilmore, Ky. : First Fruits Press, ©2015.
    Reprint. Previously published: Louisville, Ky. : Pentecostal Publishing
    Company, [1903].
    ISBN: 9781621712466 (pbk.)
    1. Methodism. 2. Sanctification. I. Title.
BT765 .S77 2015   234.8

Cover design by Wesley Wilcox & Amelia Hegle

asburyseminary.edu
800.2ASBURY
204 North Lexington Avenue
Wilmore, Kentucky 40390

First Fruits
THE ACADEMIC OPEN PRESS OF ASBURY SEMINARY

First Fruits Press

The Academic Open Press of Asbury Theological Seminary

204 N. Lexington Ave., Wilmore, KY 40390

859-858-2236

first.fruits@asburyseminary.edu

asbury.to/firstfruits

Methodism

And

The Second Blessing

BY

REV. J. C. STREET.

PENTECOSTAL PUBLISHING COMPANY,
LOUISVILLE, KY.

To My Wife
AND TO
The "Scattered and Peeled," the "Meted out
and Trodden Down," of the true Israel, Especially of the M. E. Church, North and
South; this Booklet is Affectionately Ded-
icated.

TO THE CHRISTIAN PUBLIC.

It has been my privilege to read with care the manuscript of the forth-coming book, "Methodism and The Second Blessing," by Rev. J. C. Street.

The book is needed, and for two years I have been impressed to write such a book myself. But there is no need of any other author entering this field now, for the work has been nobly done and the subject adequately treated. Few men with wide experience in authorship would have produced so good a book on this subject.

The author reveals the true literary instinct. In the spirit of a real historian he has hidden and lost himself in his work. He has not wasted a line. Like a profound lawyer, pleading a case before a Supreme Court, he has marshalled the cogent and relentless facts in massive array, bringing the reader to a resistless conclusion.

This little book is interesting, eloquent, conclusive, final, and deserves to become a classic in Methodism.　　　　　　A. M. HILLS.

TESTIMONIALS.

Central Christian Advocate: "It (Methodism and the Second Blessing) is an instructive historical study, with apt quotations, and merits attention."

Christian Witness, Chicago: "We have seen nowhere else as many authorities in one volume on the subject."

J. F. Kemper, D. D., P. E. Lincoln District, Neb. Conference: "I can very cheerfully commend the new book, 'Methodism and the Second Blessing.' This book ought to be very helpful to those who are seeking the highest standard of God's grace and blessing," etc.

Pentecostal Herald: 'Probably superior to anything ever published on the subject. It sweeps the field from Wesley's time to the present,' etc.

B. Carradine, D. D.: "Its array of proof concerning the experience of Holiness as the cardinal doctrine of Methodism, is not only formidable, but absolutely overwhelming to the candid, honest mind.

Robert McIntyre, bishop M. E. Church: "The booklet called 'Methodism and the Second Blessing,' is a capital putting of the doctrine of sanctification as held by the founders and fathers of our church. This glorious experience of the 'Double Cure' is not so well known as it should be and I wish this brochure could be studied by every Methodist preacher."

PREFACE.

We have long felt the need of such a publication as this.

If we could have had such a one placed in our hands soon after receiving the grace upheld herein, it would have saved us from much anxiety of heart if not from some spiritual failures.

We were often met with the statement that it was a "new" doctrine; or that it was not "Methodistic;" and as we were not familiar with the subject, it was difficult to meet these objections. As time went on a burden seemed laid upon us to prepare a collection of facts for the help of souls in similar circumstances.

We have gone to original sources for the most of our material, and have endeavored to give the author's meaning in each case. The italics and capitals in most cases are our own. The extracts can be depended upon.

This is only a compilation. We are not arguing a *theory*—simply giving facts, and such facts as cannot be disputed. There is no possible escape from the evidence. *Entire sanctification is subse-*

5

quent to regeneration, or is a "second blessing," according to the teaching of the M. E. Church. That men *have* received such a blessing in the past, and *that* they *are* receiving it in the present time, *by the hundreds,* IS AN INDISPUTABLE FACT. This leaves no room for Mudge, Huntington and others.

A Methodist preacher, above all others on the face of the earth, should be the last to deny the doctrine or persecute those who profess the grace of perfect love; but, alas! many of them seem to be the most bitter of all.

If it is from a lack of information on the subject, this compilation will give them light. If it is from an unwillingness to be holy and to suffer the reproach of Christ—God have mercy upon them! better had they never been born! For *"without holiness no man shall see the Lord."*

We send this forth with the prayer that God may use it to enlighten those who are in doubt as to a *second* experience, to comfort, strengthen and encourage those who are being unjustly persecuted because of their testimony to the power of God to save from all sin and uncleanness.

J. C. S.

University Place, Neb., Oct. 27, 1903.

5

CONTENTS

SOME OF WESLEY'S DEFINITIONS.

SIN.—"A voluntary transgression of a known law." *Plain Account, p. 68.*

INBRED SIN, OR SIN IN BELIEVERS.—"By sin, I here understand inward sin; any sinful temper, passion, or affection; such as pride, self-will, love of the world, in any kind or degree; such as lust, anger, peevishness; any disposition contrary to the mind which was in Christ." Sermon, *Sin in Believers.*

ENTIRE SANCTIFICATION.—"Entire sanctification, or Christian perfection, is neither more nor less than pure love; love expelling sin, and governing both the heart and life of a child of God." *Vol. VII, p. 82.*

CHAPTER I.

What was the position of John Wesley as to the time of the entire sanctification of the Christian? Did he, or did he not, teach that it was subsequent to regeneration, or a *second* work of grace? We will let him speak for himself.

In a conference with his preachers, held at Bristol, in 1765, he asks:

"What was the rise of Methodism?" and answers it thus;—"In 1729, my brother and I read the Bible; saw *inward* and *outward* holiness therein; followed after it, and incited others so to do. In 1737, we saw this holiness comes by faith. In 1738 we saw we must be *justified* BEFORE we are sanctified. But still *holiness* was our point; *inward* and outward holiness. God then thrust us out to raise a *holy people.*"

Two things are noticeable in this statement:

1. They saw that the Bible demanded both *outward* and *inward* holiness.

2.   That sanctification, or this holiness, was subsequent to justification, or a *"second blessing."*

Wesley differed from the Church of England in a number of points. Among other things he says:

"They speak of justification, either as the same thing with sanctification, or as something consequent upon it. *I believe justification to be wholly distinct from sanctification and necessarily antecedent to it."* Vol. III. p. 153.

(He includes regeneration in the term justification).

In his Journal we read of a Mr. Moltner, who contended that there were no *degrees* in faith, consequently he that had *any* faith at all, was not only justified but had a clean heart also. Wesley bewails the awful havoc this teaching had made in the society. He says he went to visit a Mr. St.——who was led away with this doctrine, and was at once met by the statement from him, "that no one has *any* degree of faith till he is *perfect as God is perfect."* In other words, he means that they are wholly sanctified the moment they believe in God, being both justified and sanctified at one and the same time.

Wesley asked him, "Have you then *no* degree of

faith?" He said, "No; for I have not a *clean heart."* Wesley then turned to the man's servant and said, "Esther, have you a clean heart?" She answered, "No; my heart is desperately wicked; but I have no doubt or fear. I know my Savior loves me; and I love him. I feel it every moment." Wesley says, "I then plainly told her master; "Here is an end of your reasoning. *This* is the state, the existence of which you deny." Vol. 3, pp. 182-3, 1740.

Mr. Wesley contends here for three things; (1) there are degrees of faith; (2) we are not wholly sanctified at the time of our justification, and (3) a mixed state of heart between justification and the time of receiving a clean heart.

On May 5th, 1740, he says: "I expounded those words, 'I write unto you, little children, because your sins are forgiven you;' and described the state of those who have forgiveness of sins, *but have not yet a clean heart."* Vol. 3, p. 183.

On August 10, 1740, he writes: "From Gal. 6:3, I earnestly warned all who had tasted the grace of God, (1) Not to think they were justified, *before* they had a *clear assurance* that God had forgiven their sins; bringing in a *calm peace, the love of God, and dominion over sin.* (2) Not to think themselves anything after they had this; but to press forward for the prize of their high calling, even a *clean heart, thoroughly* renewed after the image of God, in righteousness and true holiness." Vol. 3, p. 191.

How could the fact of a second attainment be more clearly set forth than in the above extract?

Again in a letter to a friend he makes some strong criticisms of the teaching of the Moravian church on certain points of doctrine. He says, "I do not admire their doctrine in the particulars that follow:" . . . (4) That there is no such thing as *degrees* in faith, or weak faith, since for he has no faith who has any doubt or fear. (5) *That we are sanctified wholly, the moment we are justified*; and are neither more nor less holy to the day of our death." Vol. 3, p. 52.

This is too plain for comment. Entire sanctification is a subsequent work of grace.

On April 16, 1757, an account is given of one who was justified and had peace with God, and was afterwards convinced of the need of entire holiness of heart; and how on August 23, 1744, she received the blessing while musing and praying. She says, "At that instant I felt an entire change. I was full of love, and full of God. I had the witness in myself, that he had made an end of sin, and taken my whole heart forever. And from that moment I have never lost the witness, nor felt anything in my heart but pure love." Vol. 3, pp. 624-5.

Notice, (1) She received the blessing *after* she was justified and had peace with God. (2) She has enjoyed it for about thirteen years,—from 1744 to 1757.

On May 1757 an account is given of a Miss Berresford who had lately died. She was clearly justified and became a pattern of piety and industry. She became sick. The narrator says: "When her weakness confined her to her room, she rejoiced with joy unspeakable; more especially when she was delivered from all her doubts concerning Christian perfection. Never was any one more at thirst for this, for the whole mind that was in Christ. And she earnestly exhorted all her brethren to press after it." One asked her, "Have you lately felt any remains of sin in you?" She said: "I felt pride some weeks ago." He adds, "And it seems this was the last time." "Tell all from me," she cried, "that perfection *is* attainable; and exhort all to press after it." Again she said, "Send to Mr. W—— and tell him I am sorry I did not sooner believe the doctrine of perfect holiness. Blessed be God, I now know it to be the truth." Vol. 3, p. 626.

On February 16, 1760, Wesley says he received a remarkable account from Yorkshire. About thirty persons had met together to pray and exhort one another. "After prayer was ended, when they proceeded to speak of the several states of their souls, some with deep sighs and groans complained of the burden they felt for the *remains of indwelling sin;* seeing in a clearer light than ever before, the necessity of a deliverance from it."

A part went home while some remained. While these were in prayer several were delivered and declared God did cleanse their hearts from sin.

"The next evening they met again; and the Lord was present to heal the broken in heart. One received *remission of sins;* and three more believed God had *cleansed* them from all *sin.*" Vol. 4, p. 252.

On March 6, 1760, he gives the account of two others who give a clear testimony to their justifica-

tion, and of their receiving the blessing of sancti-
cation afterwards, and now seem to be filled with
pure love. He then says, "I observe the spirit and
experience of these two run exactly paralell. Constant communion with God the Father and the
Son fills their hearts with humble love. Now this
is what I always did, and do now, mean by perfection. *And this I believe many have attained,* ON
THE SAME EVIDENCE THAT I BELIEVE MANY ARE
JUSTIFIED. May God increase their number a
thousand fold!" Vol. 4, p. 53.

On Feb. 27, 1761, he says, "At twelve I met
about thirty persons who had experienced a deep
work of God; and I appointed an hour for meeting them every week. Whether they are saved
from sin or no, they are certainly full of faith and
love, and are peculiarly helpful to my soul." Vol.
4, p. 91.

Again on March 6, "I met again those who believe God has delivered them from the root of bitterness. Their number increases daily. I know
not if fifteen or sixteen have not received the
blessing this week." Vol. 4, u. 91.

May 21, 1761, he says: "Inquiring how it was
that in all these parts we had so few witnesses of

full salvation, I constantly received one and the same answer, 'We see now, we sought it by our own works; we thought it was to come *gradually;* we never expected to receive it in a *moment,* by faith, as we did justification." Vol. 4, p. 100.

These facts are apparent: (1) Sanctification is not by growth. (2) *It is received instantly, by faith, as was justification.*

On July 23, 1761, he gives this testimony of a woman to whom he spoke personally: "She said, 'a few days before Easter last, I was deeply convinced of sin; and in Easter week I knew my sins were forgiven, and was filled with joy and peace in believing; But in about eighteen days, I was convinced, in a dream, of the necessity of a higher salvation; and I mourned day and night, in agony of desire to be *thoroughly sanctified;* till on the 23d day *after my justification,* I found a *total* change, together with a *clear witness,* that the blood of Jesus had cleansed me from all unrighteousness." Vol. 4, p. 104.

Time is not a necessary element in order to entire sanctification.

On August 4, 1762, he says, "The next morning I spoke severally with those who believe they were sanctified. They were fifty-one in all; twenty-one men, twenty-one widows or married women, and nine young women or children. In one of these the change was wrought *three weeks* after she was justified; in three, *seven days* after it, in one, *five days;* and in Susan Lutwich, age fourteen, *two days* only." Vol. 4, p. 134.

On August 6, 1762, at Macclesfield, Wesley met a number who believed the blood of Christ had cleansed them from all sin. He says: "I spoke to these (forty in all) *one by one.* Some of them said they received that blessing *ten days,* some *seven,* some *four,* some *three days* AFTER they found peace with God; *and two of them the* NEXT *day.* What marvel since one day is with God as a thousand years." Vol. 4, p. 135.

In a letter to a friend, August 27, 1768, he says: "Nay, it is true still further, that many serious, humble, sober-minded believers, who *do* feel the love of God sometimes, and do then rejoice in God their Savior, cannot be content with this; but pray continually, that he would enable them to love, and 'rejoice in the Lord always.' And no fact under heaven is more undeniable, than that God does answer this prayer; that he does, for the sake of his Son, and through the power of his Spirit, enable one and another so to do. IT IS ALSO A PLAIN FACT, THAT THIS POWER DOES COMMONLY OVERSHADOW THEM IN AN INSTANT; and that from that time they enjoy that inward and outward holiness, to which they were utter strangers before." . . . . . .

"Many *think* they are justified, and *are not*; but we cannot infer, that *none are justified. So neither, if many think they are 'perfected in love' and are not, will it follow that none are so.* Blessed be God, though we set a hundred enthusiasts (fanatics) aside, we are still 'encompassed with a cloud of witnesses,' who have testified, and do testify, in life and in death, that perfection which I have taught these forty years! This perfection cannot be a delusion, unless the Bible is a delusion too; I mean loving God with all our heart and our neighbor as ourselves. I pin down all its opposers to this definition." Vol. 4, p. 289.

I wish to call attention to *six* facts contained in the above letter:

1.   Those who love God now, are praying for *perfect love.*

2. God answers their prayer and gives them their desire.

3. It is done *instantly*.

4. Because some think they are sanctified, but are not, is no reason for rejecting all who profess it; any more than those who think they are justified but are not, should cause us to reject all who *say* they are justified.

5. A cloud of witnesses remain after all *false* professors are set aside.

6. He has preached this perfection,—namely, entire sanctification, as a second work of grace enabling qne to love God with all the heart,—for forty years,—or from the beginning of his career.

In the "Further Thoughts" published in 1759, these questions are found:

"Q. But what if none have attained it yet? What if all who think so are deceived?"

"A. Convince me of this, and I will preach it no more. But understand me right; *I do not build any doctrine on this or that person.* This or any other man may be deceived, and I am not moved. But if there are none made perfect yet, God has not sent me to preach perfection." . . . .

"Q. But what does it signify, whether any have attained it or no, seeing so many Scriptures witness for it?"

"A. If I were convinced that none in England had attained what has been so clearly and strongly preached by such a number of preachers, in so many places, and for so long a time, I should be clearly convinced that we had all mistaken the meaning of those Scriptures; and, therefore for the time to come, I too, must teach that "sin will remain till death." *Plain Account,"* pp. 89-91.

It has been asserted by some, that Wesley was too credulous, and that he laid too much stress upon individual testimony, and because of this was led into a wrong position in doctrine. Does not the above refute such? *He did not build upon the experience of "this or that person."* He used a strictly scientific method in reaching his conclusions concerning this doctrine. In the *"Plain Account,"* p. 45, he says, "Indeed by viewing it in every point of light, and comparing it again and again with the Word of God on the one hand, and the experience of the chilrren of God on the other, we saw farther into the nature and properties of Christian perfection."

He was as careful as any scientist in *his* examinations of natural phenomena. He did not hastily form an opinion from the testimony of a *few,* but put a *multitude* of witnesses to as severe a test as any lawyer could before a court of justice.

As an illustration of this, I wish to quote from his Journal for December 2, 1744: "I was with two persons who believed they are saved from all sin. Be it so, or not, why should we not rejoice in the work of God, so far as it is unquestionably wrought in them? For instance, I ask John C., 'Do you pray always? Do you rejoice in God every moment? Do you in everything give thanks? In loss? In pain? In sickness, weariness, disappointments? Do you desire nothing? Do you fear nothing? Do you feel the love of God continually in your heart? Have you a witness in whatever you speak or do, that it is pleasing God?' If he can solemnly and deliberately answer in the affirmative, why do I not rejoice and praise God on his behalf? Perhaps, because I have an exceeding complex idea of sanctification, or a sanctified man. And so, for fear he should not have attained all I include in that idea, I cannot rejoice in what he has attained." Vol. 3, p. 323.

At other times he and others asked these persons the most searching questions they could devise. He was not credulous, but rather incredulous, as the above quotation seems to indicate. He was careful and discriminating, and a logician of the first order.

Macauley characterizes him as, "a man whose eloquence and logical acuteness might have ren-dered him eminent in literature, whose genius for government was not inferior to that of Richelieu."

Such a man was not likely to form hasty conclu-sions, nor follow a false doctrine. He desired truth, and did not hesitate to follow the light as it was given. He gave up all that men count dear, that he might gain Christ.

Some may say he was only a mistaken enthusi-ast, and taught the doctrine of inbred sin, and en-tire sanctification as a *second* work of grace be-cause of the false ideas and theories in the psychol-ogy of that time. But Wesley did not base his doc-trine of inbred sin upon any one's psychology or philosophy, or upon any individual's experience, but upon the Word of God and the experience of the children of God, of the past and of the then present time. He was not so foolish as to build his hopes of an enternity with God on the speculations of men,—(and psychology contains much speculation)—but upon the eternal word of God, —upon a teaching wrought out through prayer and fasting,—a teaching, the experience of which has stood the test of the trials of life and the awful ordeal of death.

His critics will be remembered only by the fact that they have crossed swords with him, while his name will continue to shine even with a brighter luster, and the doctrine which he emphasized will continue to lead souls to a union with God in perfect love until the end of time.

He saw from the Bible and the experience of Christians, that even those who had peace with God, were still burdened with a nature not in complete harmony with holiness and God, and needed a further work of grace, even the circumcision of the heart, in order that they might love God with all their heart.

CHAPTER II.

John Wesley did not hesitate to attack error wherever he preceived it,—especially if the error concerned vital religion.

On March 28, 1763, he says, "I retired to Lewisham, and wrote the sermon on 'Sin in Believers,' in order to remove a mistake which some were laboring to propagate,—that there is no sin in any that are justified." Vol. 4, p. 147.

To avoid any misunderstanding of his terms we quote this from the above sermon, "I use indifferently the words *regenerate, justified,* or *believers;* . . . . as every one that believes, is *both* justified and born of God." Vol. 1, p. 109.

He defines this remaining sin as "any sinful temper, passion, or affection; such as pride, self-will, love of the world, in any kind or degree; such as lust, anger, peevishness; any disposition contrary to the mind which was in Christ." Vol. 1, p. 109.

24

In this sermon on "Sin in Believers" he says: "I cannot therefore by any means receive this assertion, that there is no sin in a believer from the moment he is justified; *first,* because it is contrary to the whole tenor of Scripture; *second,* because it is contrary to the experience of the children of God; *thirdly,* because it is absolutely new, never heard of in the world till yesterday; and *lastly,* because it is naturally attended with the most fatal consequences."

Count Zinzendorf, through the Moravian church, was teaching that all were wholly sanctified at the same moment with justification. Wesley opposed this with all his might for the reasons in the quotations last given.

Some may say that Wesley gave regeneration a small place in order to make room for his doctrine of sin in believers. Let us see what he says on this. We quote from his sermon on "Repentance in Believers," found in the first volume of sermons: "We allow, that, at the very moment of justification, we are 'born again,' in that instant we experience that inward change, 'from darkness into marvelous light; from the image of the brute and the devil, into the image of God; from the earthly, sensual, devilish mind to the mind which was in Christ Jesus. But are we then entirely changed? are we *wholly* transformed into the image of Him who created us? *Far from it;* we still retain a depth of sin, and it is the consciousness of this, which constrains us to groan for a full deliverance, to Him that is mighty to save. Hence it is, that those believers who are not convinced of the deep corruption of their own hearts; but slightly, and as it were, notionally convinced, have little concern about entire sanctification." Vol. 1, p. 124.

He does not degrade regeneration, but rather exalts it. It meant a *complete deliverance from sinning,* with him. This is as high a standard for regeneration as some teach for sanctification,— Keswickism, for instance.

But this is not to our point. Wesley held that we were not entirely sanctified at the time of our regeneration, but were delivered from the remains of sin by a *second* work of grace.

We quote again from his sermon *"Repentance in Believers:"* "Though we watch and pray ever so much, we can not wholly cleanse either our hearts or hands. Most sure we cannot till it shall please our God to speak the second *time* 'Be clean,' and then only the leprosy is **cleansed.** Then only, the evil root, the carnal mind, is **no** more. *But if there be no* SECOND CHANGE, if there be no *instantaneous* deliverance AFTER justification, if there be *none but* a gradual work of God, (that there is a gradual work none denies) then we must be content, as well as we can, to remain full of sin till death."

Notice these facts in the above:

1. We can not sanctify ourselves by works, **or** in other words, we can't *grow* sin out.

2. God cleanses by a *second* work.

3. Inbred sin is taken away.

4. It is done *instantaneously,* connected with **a** gradual work.

A letter written to Mr. Joseph Benson, Dec. 28, 1770, is so remarkable and to the point, we quote at length from it.

"One point I advise you to hold fast, and let neither men nor devils tear it from you. You are a child of God; you are justified freely through the redemption which is in Christ Jesus. Your sins are forgiven! Cast not away that confidence, etc. . . Now, can any be justified, but by faith? None can. Therefore, you are a believer; you have faith in Christ; you *know* the Lord; you can say 'My Lord and my God;' and whoever denies this, may as well deny that the sun shines at noonday.

> "Yet still ten thousand lusts remain,
>   And vex your soul absolved from sin;
> Still rebel nature strives to reign,
>   And you are all unclean, unclean!

"This is equally clear and undeniable. And this is not only *your* experience, *but the experience of a thousand believers beside, who yet are as sure of God's favor, as of their own existence.* To cut off all doubt on this head, I beg you to give another serious reading to those two sermons, '*Sin in Believers*' and '*Repentance of Believers*'.

"But is there no help? Is there no deliverance, no salvation from this inbred enemy?   Surely there is, else many great and precious promises must fall to the ground.   Then will I sprinkle clean water upon you, and ye shall be clean; from all your filthiness, and from all your idols, will I cleanse you." Eze. 36:25, etc.

"And the Lord thy God will circumcise thine heart, and the heart of thy seed, to love the Lord thy God with all thine heart, etc." Deut. 30:6.

This I term sanctification, (which is both an instantaneous and a gradual work) or perfection, the being perfected in love, filled with love, which still admits of a thousand degrees. But I have no time to throw away in contending for words; especially when the *thing* is allowed. And you allow the whole thing which I contend for; *an entire deliverance from sin,* a recovery of the whole image of God, the loving God with all our heart, soul, and strength. And you believe God is able to give you this; yea, to give it you in an instant. You trust he will. O hold fast this also; this blessed hope, which he has wrought in your heart; and with all zeal and diligence confirm the brethren, (1.) In holding fast that whereto they have attained; namely, the remission of all their sins, by faith in a bleeding Lord; (2.) *In expecting a* SECOND CHANGE, *whereby they shall be saved from all sin and perfected in love."* Vol. 7, p. 71.

This letter contains these facts, among others:

1. Sin—inbred sin (as defined by him above) remains in those who are as sure of their justification as of their own existence.

2. That there may be an instantaneous deliverance from this inbred enemy, or else many promises fail.

3. He calls it a SECOND CHANGE, thus indicating its relation to justification.

Men may ridicule the phrase, the *"Second Blessing,"* but is not the term as Scriptural as the more common one, of "conversion?" We hold that it is; but we do not contend for a term. Wesley used it frequently, so that it is both Wesleyan and Methodistic.

In a letter to Mrs. Crosby, dated Feb. 14, 1761, Wesley says: "I believe within five weeks, six in one class have received remission of sins, and five in one band received a SECOND BLESSING." Vol. 7, p. 28.

Again, to a Miss Hilton, he writes: "Do you now feel anything like anger, or pride, or self-will, or any remains of the carnal mind? Was your SECOND deliverance wrought while I was at Beverly? At the time of the sermon or after it?" Vol. 7, p. 41, 1769.

He writes again to the same person, now Mrs. Barton, Oct. 8, 1774, "It is exceeding certain God did give you the SECOND BLESSING, *properly so called.* He delivered you from the root of bitterness, from *inbred,* as well as *actual* sin." Vol. 7, p. 45.

These quotations alone, are sufficient to prove to any candid mind that Wesley believed in, and taught, a SECOND BLESSING, but in order that none shall have an excuse, we will give a few more quotations showing that Wesley held this doctrine till the day of his death:

In a letter to Miss H. A. Roe, Jan. 7, 1782, he says: "In the success of Mr. Leech's preaching, we have one proof of a thousand, that *the blessing of God always attends the publishing of* FULL SAL-VATION *as attainable* NOW, *by simple faith.* You should always have in readiness that little tract, *"The Plain Account of Christian Perfection."* There is nothing that would so effectually stop the mouths of those who call this a 'new doctrine.' All who thus object are really (though they suspect nothing less) seeking sanctification by works. If it be by works, then certainly these will need time, in order to the doing of these works. But if it is by faith, it is plain, a moment is as a thousand years. Then God says, (in the spiritual, as in the outward world), 'Let there be light, and there is light.' . . . . .

"A few witnesses of pure love remain, there (at Macclesfield) still; . . . . .

Encourage those in M.—— who enjoy it; to speak explicitly what they do experience; and to go on, till they know all that 'love of God that passeth knowledge'." Vol. 7, p. 195.

Notice he, (1) Approves the preaching of full salvation receivable now, by simple faith.

2.   Declares God's blessing always attends it.

3.   Recommends the "Plain Account," written about twenty years before.

4.   Those who have this blessing should explicitly testify to it.

In a letter to a Miss Cooke, Sept. 9, 1785, he writes: "You have tasted of the love of God. See that you do not cast it away. See that you hold fast he beginning of your confidence steadfast unto the end! And how soon may you be made partaker of sanctification! *And not only by a slow and insensible growth in grace, but by the power of the highest overshadowing you, in a* MOMENT, *in the* TWINKLING *of an eye, so as utterly to abolish sin, and to renew you in his whole image!* If you are simple of heart, if you are willing to receive the heavenly gift as a little child, without reasoning, why may you not receive it *now?* He is nigh that sanctifieth; he is with you; he is knocking at the door of your heart!" Vol. 7, p. 198.

While at Redruth on Sept. 27, 1785, he says: "At our love feast in the evening, several of our friends declared how God had saved them from *inbred sin,* with such exactness, both of sentiment, and language, as clearly showed they were taught of God." Vol. 4, p. 624.

In a letter to Freeborn Garretson in 1785, he says: "And it will be well, as soon as any of them find peace with God, to exhort them to go on to perfection! *The more explicitly and strongly you press all believers to aspire after full sanctification, as attainable now by simple faith, the more the whole work of God will prosper."* Vol. 7, p. 184.

He says of the society at St. Margaret's, May 7, 1786, "I have not for many years known this society in so prosperous a condition. This is undoubtedly owing, first, to the exact discipline which has for some time been observed among them; and, next, *to the strongly and continually*

exhorting the believers to 'go on to perfection'."
Vol. 4, p. 632.

In his Journal for Feb. 6, 1789, he writes of
meeting the local preachers, and says, "Taking the
opportunity of having them all together, at the
watch-night, I strongly insisted on St. Paul's ad-
vice to Timothy, 'Keep that which is committed to
thy trust;' *particularly the doctrine of Christian
Perfection, which God has peculiarly entrusted to
the Methodists.*" Vol. 4, p. 712.

On March 13, 1790, he writes: "This week I
visited the classes in Bristol. I wonder we do not
increase in number, although many are convinced, .
many justified, and a few perfected in love."
Vol. 4, p. 737.

On June 17, 1780, in speaking of the society at
Hutton Rudby, he says: "Twenty years this society was a pattern to all the country for serious-
ness and deep devotion. I think seventeen of them
were *perfected in love.*" Vol. 4, p. 743.

On Sept. 15, 1790, in a letter to Robt. Brack-
enbury, Esq., he says: "I am glad Brother D——
has more light with regard to *full sanctification.
This doctrine is the grand depositum which God
has lodged with the people called Methodists; and*

for the sake of propagating this chiefly he ap-peared to have raised us up." Vol. 7, p. 153.

In a letter to Adam Clarke, Nov. 26, 1790, about *three months* before Wesley's death, he thus writes: "To retain the grace of God is much more than to gain it; hardly one in three does this. And this should be strongly and explicitly urged on all who have tasted of *perfect love. If we can prove that any of our local preachers or leaders, either directly or indirectly, speak against it, let him be a local preacher or leader no longer. I doubt whether he should continue in the society.* Because he that could thus speak in our congre-gations cannot be an honest man." Vol. 7. p 206.

Hear it, all ye Methodists! Hear it, all ye preachers, who stand before the conference bar and declare before God and man that you "are going on unto perfection," and "expect to be made per-fect in love in this life," and declare you believe the doctrines of the M. E. church, and will "preach and maintain them," and now ridicule, persecute and discount those who obtain and testify to this very grace you have sworn to seek and to sup-port! Hear it, from the lips of the founder of Methodism three months ere his spirit returned to

God,—*"that he that could thus speak against this doctrine cannot be an honest man!"* God have mercy upon the traitors in Methodism!

In a letter to Mr. Edward Lewly, Jan. 12, 1791, about two months before his death, he says,—"A man that is not a thorough friend to Christian Perfection will easily puzzle others, and thereby weaken, if not destroy, any select society." Vol. 7, p. 253.

There is no appearance of a change in his sentiments concerning this great doctrine, but from the borders of the grave comes his voice still defending it. He died on March 2, 1791. In a letter to Mr. John Booth, dated Jan. 29, 1791, only thirty-two days before his death, he says, "Whenever you have apportunity of speaking to *believers, urge them to go on to perfection.* Spare no pains; and God, our own God, still give you his blessing." Vol. 7. p. 238.

One more quotation from this apostolical man and we close this part of our labor. On Feb. 27, in the evening, only three days before his death, he said, "We must be justified by faith, *and then go on to full sanctification."* Stevens History Methodism, Vol. 2, p. 371.

Many more quotations might be given; but is not this sufficient?

Surely no normal human mind can resist the evidence given.

These facts are evident from the quotations above.

1. Wesley believed and taught the fact of "inbred sin." (See his definition).

2. That this remained in the regenerate.

3. That this is removed in entire sanctification.

4. That entire sanctification is a SECOND *change* or *blessing,* thus coming *after* justification and regeneration.

5. That entire sanctification may be obtained by faith, as was justification, and consequently instantaneously .

6. He maintained the same doctrine to the day of his death.

CHAPTER III.

Historic Proof.

In his Centenary Address, Dr. John McClintock makes this far-reaching and thought-arousing statement: "Knowing exactly what I say, and taking the full responsibility of it, I repeat, we are the only church in history, from the Apostles' time until now, that has put forth as its very elemental thought the great, central, prevailing idea of the whole book of God from the beginning to the end—*the holiness of the human soul, heart, mind, and will.*"

Dr. Warren, of Boston University, says in his Introduction to Theology,—"In Luther's mind, justification by faith was the central idea of Christianity, and in Calvin's the decree was the central idea. But Methodism, in respect to its inmost spirit and essence, is a viewing of Christianity from the standpoint of Christian perfection, or perfect love."

In his "History of American Methodism," Dr.

Stevens says, "The holy club was formed at Oxford in 1729 for the sanctification of its members. The Wesleys there sought personal purification, * * * *. Geo. Whitefield joined them for the same purpose." p. 25.

"For his doctrine of sanctification Wesley adopted the title of 'Perfection,' because he found it so used in the Holy Scriptures. Paul and John he deemed sufficient authorities for the use of the epithet, which he knew, however, would be liable to the cavils of criticism." Hist. M. E. Church, Vol. 2, p. 212.

Wesley's theory of the doctrine is precise and intelligible, though often distorted into perplexing difficulties by both its advocates and opponents. He taught not absolute, nor angelic, nor Adamic, but Christian perfection." Ibid. p. 213.

After describing more fully Wesley's doctrine, Dr. Stevens, says: "Is there such a thing as the inspired writer calls 'perfect love' which 'casteth out fear?' (I Jno. 4:18). Wesley believed that there is; that it is the privilege of all saints; and that it is to be attained by faith." Ibid. p. 215.

In the *History of Methodism,* Vol. I, Dr. Stevens says: "During forty years he (Wesley) had been preaching, as he says, this doctrine of Christian Perfection, and throughout that period many exemplary witnesses of it lived and died in his societies." p. 405.

Speaking of the spread of this doctrine through the itinerants, Stevens says of them: "Every one of them, at his reception into the traveling ministry, avows his belief in the doctrine, and that he is "groaning after," if he has not already attained, this exalted grace. *Perhaps no single fact affords a better explanation of the marvelous success of Methodism.* Wesley observed and declared that wherever it was preached revivals usually prevailed." p. 405-06.

"The doctrine of personal sanctification was, in fine, the great potential idea of Methodism." p. 406. "Wesley defined this Scripture truth more clearly than any other modern writer. Evangelical theologians cannot deny his definition of the doctrine." They can differ only as to the time it is attained.

"Wesley claimed it as, like justification, an attainment of faith, and practicable at any moment." p. 406.

In particularizing Wesley's doctrines, Dr. Stevens, in his *History of Methodism,* Vol. II. p. 411, says:

"He discriminates three stages, or rather three distinctions, in the personal experience of the 'great salvation' thus provided.

"Justification is distinguished from regeneration only logically. It is a relative fact—a work done for us rather than in us—the pardon of sin, whereby the relation of the sinner to the Divine law is changed, and he is recognized, through the Atonement, as no longer guilty, but just, and has 'peace with God through our Lord Jesus Christ.'

"Regeneration is a work wrought by the Holy Spirit in the believing soul, whereby it passes from death unto life, and receiving 'the spirit of adoption,' enters into communion with God."

"Sanctification, as a doctrine, received peculiar illustration and enforcement from Wesley, and the standard Methodist writers generally. IT IS THE PURIFICATION OF THE BELIEVER SUBSEQUENTLY TO REGENERATION. It is usually gradual; but may be *instantaneous,* as like justification, it is received by faith, * * * * *. But this experience, he taught, should be sought *immediately*; and as it is obtained by faith, it is the privilege of all believers at any time."

These extracts from Dr. Stevens are sufficient to show that Wesley believed in and taught a *second work* of grace, and that only as we keep to that doctrine are we truly Methodists.

In the *"Life of Adam Clarke,"* by J. B. B. Clarke, we find his *creed* given.

Article XVIII., which succeeds the one on regeneration is as follows:

"The souls of all *believers* may be purified from all sin in this life; and man may live under the continual influence of the grace of Christ, so as not to sin against God. *All sinful tempers and evil propensities being destroyed,* and his heart constantly filled with pure love both to God and man." Vol. I. p. 150.

In *"Everett's Life of Clarke,* we find this, which was spoken to a friend who was misinformed as to Clark's views on entire sanctification:

"As to the words which you quote as mine, I totally disclaim them. I never said; I never intended to say them. *I believe justification and sanctification to be widely distinct works."*

He, like Wesley, includes *regeneration* in the term *justification.*

Again in the same book, he says, "I have been twenty-three years a traveling preacher, and have been acquainted with some thousands of Christians during that time, who were in different states of grace; and *I never, to my knowledge, met with a single individual where God both justified and sanctified at the same time."*

Tyreman says: "The doctrine of Christian Perfection, attainable in one instant by a simple act of faith, *was made prominent* in Methodist congregations in 1762, and ever after it was one of the chief topics of Mr. Wesley's ministry and that of his itinerant preachers." Vol. II. pp. 346, 416, 444.

Again he says in a letter to a Mr. Estes, "All who are acquainted with Methodist history are well aware that Methodism has always prospered most when the doctrine of entire sanctification has been most popular."

Dr. Bangs says, in his History of the M. E. Church, "The doctrine more especially urged upon believers (in early Methodism) was that of *sanctification* or *holiness* of heart and life, and this was *pressed* upon them as their *present* privilege, depending for its accomplishment *now* on the faithfulness of God, who had promised to do it. It was this baptism of the Holy Ghost which fired and filled the hearts of God's ministers at that time."

Again in an article in the "Guide to Holiness" (now the "Consecrated Life") in 1854, Dr. Bangs said: "Those who teach that we are gradually to grow into a state of sanctification, without ever experiencing an *instantaneous* change from inbred sin to holiness,—*are to be repudiated as unsound, anti-scriptural and anti-Wesleyan.*"

In Bishop Asbury's Journal, Vol. I. p. 214, from an article under the caption, *"A Brief Narrative of the Revival of Religion in Va.,"* written, I judge, by Mr. Jarratt, we take the following extract:

"One of the doctrines, as you know, which we particularly insist upon, is that of a present salvation; a salvation not only from the guilt and power, but also from the root of sin; a cleansing from all filthiness of flesh and spirit, that we may perfect holiness in the fear of God; a going on to perfection, which we sometimes define by loving God with all our hearts. Several who had believed were deeply sensible of their want of this. I have seen both men and women, who had long been happy in a sense of God's pardoning love, as much convicted on account of the remains of sin in their hearts, and as much distressed for a total deliverance from them, *as ever I saw any for justification.* * * * * *. And I have been present when they believed that God answered (their) prayer, and bestowed this blessing upon them. I have conversed with them several times since, and have found them thoroughly devoted to God. They all testify, that they have received the gift *instantaneously,* and by simple faith. We have sundry witnesses of this perfect love who are above all suspicion. I have known the men and their communication for many years, and have ever found them zealous for the cause of God—men of sense and integrity, patterns of piety and humility; whose testimony, therefore, may be depended upon.

This gives a clear conception of the doctrine as it was taught them, (1776)—a *second* crisis in the religious experience—a cleansing from inbred sin, and enabling them to love God with all the heart.

Much more might be given from history, but this is sufficient to sustain our proposition.

CHAPTER IV.

Singing was one of the characteristics of early Methodism. Naturally the sentiment of her songs was formed by her theology, so that the gospel of a free and full salvation was not only preached, but also, sung into the hearts of the people. The Hymnal, then, becomes a strong witness to the doctrine of entire sanctification as a work of grace *subsequent* to regeneration.

If you will examine the hymnal you will notice that the hymns are all classified under certain topics. Beginning with number 377 we have hymns on Repentance. These are followed by those on *justification* and *Adoption.* These by *Consecration* hymns; and then comes those on *Sanctification* and *Growth,* etc.

Please notice the order of arrangement: repentance, justification and adoption; consecration, sanctification and growth. The order, or stages of the process of salvation, seems to be indicated by

47

this arrangement. Repentance leads to justification and adoption; this is followed by consecration—the condition of receiving perfect love—purity of heart, or entire sanctification.

There are altogether *seventy-one* hymns on the subject of Sanctification and Growth; while Repentance has *forty* only and Justification and Adoption only *fifty-six*. Out of the seventy-one, forty were composed by Chas. Wesley; six were translated and adopted by John Wesley, leaving only twenty-five to other writers.

Notice the difference in the sentiment of the hymns under the several topics.

In those under Repentance we hear the cry of a penitent for forgiveness. Under Justification and Adoption, it is the rejoicing of one over sins forgiven and a God reconciled; while those under Sanctification and Growth express the desire of the child of God for purity, perfect love, or the whole image of God. This difference is very apparent.

The hymns that we shall examine are those that voice the desire of the child of God for a full deliverance from those hindrances within that tend to keep him from loving God with all his heart.

Number 545 is based upon Matt. 5:3, 6, and 8, respectively.

The first verse is a plea for pardon; the second for the "hunger and thirst for righteousness" that comes to the true child of God only. The third verse we give in full:

> "Jesus the *crowning* grace impart;
> Bless me with purity of heart,
>   That now beholding thee,
> I soon may view thy open face,
> On all thy glorious beauties gaze,
>   And God forever see."

In the first stanza it is forgiveness that is craved, in the last the *"crowning grace,"* of purity of heart.

In hymn number 529, the first two stanzas are based upon I Thess. 4:3,—"This is the will of God, *even* your sanctification," and the last two upon Deut. 30:6, "And the Lord thy God will circumcise thy heart * * * to love the Lord thy God with all thy heart etc."

> "1.   He wills that I should holy be,
>   That holiness I long to feel;

That full divine conformity,
    To all my Saviour's righteous will.

"3.   On thee, O Lord my soul is stayed
    And waits to prove thine utmost will;
The promise by thy mercy made,
    Thou canst, thou wilt, in me fulfill."

"4.   No more I stagger at thy power,
    Or doubt thy truth, which cannot move;
Hasten the long expected hour,
    And bless me with thy perfect love."

Hymns 525 and 528 are parts of one hymn by
C. Wesley, originally containing twenty-eight stanzas.   It was entitled *"Pleading the Promise of
Sanctification,"* and is founded upon Eze. 36:23-
31.

The fourth stanza of No. 528 as it stands in the
Hymnal is thus:

"O that I now, from sin released,
    Thy word may to the utmost prove;
Enter into the promised rest,
    The Canaan of thy perfect love!"

It is only necessary to refer to No. 521, beginning,—"O for a heart to praise my God, A heart from sins set free," etc. Any one can at once see that the cry is not for pardon, but for a clean—a perfect heart. This hymn is based upon Ps. 51:10.

Number 519 was entitled by Chas. Wesley—*"Christ our Sanctification."* It is a plea of God's child for purification from "vile affections."

We give verses three and five:

3. "More of thy life, and more I have,
    As the old Adam dies;
  Bury me, Saviour, in thy grave,
    That I with thee may rise.

5. "Scatter the *last remains of sin,*
    And seal me thine abode;
  O make me glorious all within,
    A temple built by God!"

Number 513, may also be referred to as a prayer of God's people—not sinners—for perfect rest.

"Lord I believe a rest remains,
  To all thy people known;
    *   *   *   *

"A rest where all our souls desire
　Is fixed on things above;
Where　fear　and　sin　and　grief　expire,
　Cast out by perfect love."

We quote the third verse of number 495:

　　"Break off the yoke of *inbred sin,*
　　　And fully set my spirit free;
　　I cannot rest till pure within,
　　　Till I am wholly lost in thee."

Number 493 is mutilated, as are many others.
It originally had eight stanzas, the 2nd 3rd and
5th have been omitted. We give the original 2nd
and 3rd verses.

　　"The Lord our Righteousness
　　　We have *long since* received,
　　Salvation nearer is
　　　Than　when　we　first　believed;
　　Rejoice in hope,　rejoice with　me,
　　We shall from all our sins be free.

"Let others hug their chains,
  For sins and Satan plead,
And   say   from   sin's   remains
  They never can be freed;
Rejoice in hope, etc."

We come now to number 491, a familiar and gracious hymn. The second stanza is a clear witness to a second blessing. We give it entire:

"Breathe, O Breathe thy loving Spirit,
  Into every trouble breast!
Let us all in thee inherit,
  Let us find that *second rest,*

Take away our *bent* to *sinning;*
  Alpha and Omega be;
End of faith, as its beginning,
  Set our hearts at liberty."

One more hymn and we close this part of the evidence.

Number 486 was originally entitled, *"For those that wait for full Redemption."* Only the last half is given in our hymnal. We give the second and third verses, with the first two as it now stands.

> 2. Surely I have pardon found,
>   Grace doth more than sin abound,
>   God I know is pacified,
>   Thou for me, for me, hast died;
>
> 3. But I cannot rest herein,
>   All my nature still is sin,
>   Comforted I will not be,
>   Till my soul is all like thee."
>
> 1. (4) Savior of the sin-sick soul,
>   Give me faith to make me whole;
>   Finish thy great work of grace;
>   Cut it short in righteousness
>
> 2. (5) Speak the SECOND TIME 'Be clean!'"
>   Take away my *inbred sin*;
>   Every stumbling block remove;
>   Cast it out by perfect love,"

Many others might be given expressing the cry **of** the believers heart for complete deliverance from indwelling hindrances to perfect love, but these are sufficient for our purpose. Let any one take the Hymnal and satisfy themselves.

We are indebted to *"Nutter's Hymn Studies"* for many of the above facts concerning the hymns.

CHAPTER V.

The first statement in the Discipline on the subject of holiness is found in the *"Episcopal Address."* It reads thus:

"We believe that God's design in raising up the Methodist Episcopal church in America was to evangelize the continent and spread Scriptural holiness over these lands."

The next most specific reference is found in the *"Historical Statement."* This has already been quoted but we will give a part here.

"In 1729 two young men in England, reading the Bible, saw they could not be saved without holiness, * * * * *. In 1739 they saw likewise, that men are *justified* BEFORE they are *sanctified.*"

In the last part of the Second Article of Religion, page 19, is found a statement in which a reference is made to the *double* character of the Atonement of Christ. He was " a sacrifice, not only for *original* guilt, but also for the *actual* sins of men."

Article VII defines what is meant by original guilt or sin,—"it is the corruption of the nature of every man that naturally is engendered of the offspring of Adam, whereby man is very far gone from original righteousness, and of his own nature inclined to evil, and that continually."

This is the *"inbred sin"* of which C. Wesley sings—"Break off the yoke of *inbred sin,"*—"Take away our *bent* to *sinning."* This is something that cannot be *forgiven,* for only *acts* can be forgiven. But this has been inherited as a result of Adam's loss of holiness.

It is true that our present Discipline has no article or paragraph, or section that *specifically* treats the subject of entire sanctification, or Christian perfection. It was not so in the beginning. In the Discipline adopted in 1784 it was distinctly treated in a question and answer method.

In 1787 it was made a separate section and entitled, *"Of Perfection."* We give it as found in a copy of the Discipline of 1784, published in 1791, at Philadelphia, by Joseph Crukshank.

SEC. 22. OF PERFECTION.

"Let us strongly and explicitly exhort all believers to go on to perfection. That we may all speak the same thing, we ask once for all. Shall we defend this perfection or give it up? We all agree to defend it, meaning thereby (as we did from the beginning) salvation from all sin, by the love of God and man filling our hearts. The Papists say, "This cannot be attained till we have been refined by the fire of purgatory." Some professors say, "Nay, it will be obtained as soon as the soul and body part." Others say, "It may be attained before we die;" a moment after is too late." Is it so, or not? We are all agreed, we may be saved from all sin before death, properly so called, sinful tempers, but we cannot always speak or think or act aright, as dwelling in houses of clay. The substance then is settled. But as to the circumstances, is the change gradual or instantaneous? It is both the one and the other. "But should we, in preaching, insist both on one and the other." Certainly we should insist on the gradual change, and that earnestly and continually. And are there not reasons why we should insist on the instantaneous change? If there be such a blessed change before death, should we not encourage all believers to expect it? And the rather, because constant experience shows, the more earnestly they expect this, the more swiftly and steadily does the gradual work of God go on in their souls; the more careful are they to grow in grace; the more zealous of good works, and the more punctual in their attendance on all the ordinances of God; (whereas just the contrary effects are observed, whenever this expectation ceases.) They are saved by hope, by this hope of a total change, with a gradually increasing salvation. Destroy this hope, and that salvation stands still, or rather decreases daily. *Therefore, whoever would advance the gradual change in believers should strongly insist on the instantaneous."*

This gives us a clear knowledge of the position of the M. E. church on this great subject at the very time of its origin. It was organized in 1784, and at this time the above section on *Perfection* was adopted. Five years later (1789) Wesley's *Plain Account* was added to the Discipline. These two articles, then, must be regarded as representing the mind of the church on this doctrine at this time.

The question now arises as to whether there has been any authoritative change in the doctrine since that time. We answer in the negative, and proceed to the proof.

The title on the Discipline up to the year 1792 was simply, *"A Form of Discipline For the Ministers, Preachers, and Members of the M. E. Church of America,"* with the exception that in 1790 and 1791 this parenthentical clause was inserted in the above title after the word members, namely: ("now comprehending the Principles and Doctrines.")

In 1792 the title was changed to the following: "The Doctrines and Discipline of the M. E. Church in America etc."

This edition still includes the section, *"On Perfection"* and Wesley's *"Plain Account."* Here then, is positive proof that *Perfection* as taught by Wesley—a second definite instantaneous work of grace (see chapters I and II.)—was a doctrine of the church in 1792.

In 1798 an edition of the Discipline containing explanatory notes by bishops Coke and Asbury, was published. To avoid making it too bulky, the doctrinal sections were omitted and published separately, but were again restored to their place in the Discipline in 1801, three years later, and remained there until the General Conference of 1808.

This conference adopted what is known as the *"First Restrictive Rule,"* which is a guard against doctrinal change in the Church. This rule reads as follows, *"The General Conference* shall not revoke, alter, nor change our Articles of Religion, *nor establish any new standards or rules of doctrine contrary to our* PRESENT EXISTING AND ES-TABLISHED STANDARDS OF DOCTRINE." *Discip. par. 67, sec. 1.*

We call attention to the last part, and ask, What were the then *"present existing and established standards of doctrine?"* Were they not, in part at least, the two articles referred to above, *viz. "Perfection,"* and the *"Plain Account,"* by Wesley? No other conclusion can possibly be truthfully drawn. These have represented the teaching of the church from 1784 until 1808, and were still an *"established standard"* at the time of the adoption of the above restrictive rule. *It is undeniable, then, that this doctrine, as set forth in these two articles,* (not to speak of others containing the same teaching), *had been, and were then, a standard doctrine of the church, which, by their Restrictive Rule, adopted by the General Conference of* 1808, *has* BEEN MADE UNCHANGEABLE FOREVER*!* This being true, then, entire sanctification, as a *second* blessing, is a doctrine of the M. E. Church to-day.

We will give one more proof, from the Discipline, although we do not need it to gain our case, but that all may be left "without excuse," we will take the time and space to insert it.

Every preacher who becomes a member of an Annual Conference must answer the following questions in open conference before the presiding Bishop:

1. "Have you faith in Christ?"

2. "Are you going on to perfection?"

3. "Do you expect to be made perfect in love in this life?"

4. "Are you earnestly striving after it?"

* * * *

8. "Have you studied the doctrines of the M. E. Church?"

9. "After full examination do you believe that our Doctrines are in harmony with the Holy Scriptures?"

10. "Will you preach and maintain them?"

There are nineteen questions all together, but these are all that bear upon our subject.

Some may say that it is not indicated *how* the questions are to be answered, so that one may have his own individual opinion of the matter. *Not indicated how!* John Wesley was not a man of such aimless drivel as that. He had a purpose in those questions and meant that they should be answered in the affirmative. The first four questions as they stand in our Discipline, and as given above, are, essentially, in the very words of Wesley. the others are modified or changed to suit the American conditions.

Imagine a preacher standing before the Bishop in open conference and answering questions, nine or ten in the negative, or in an indifferent manner, even,—would he be received into the conference? *Certainly not.*

It is certain, also, that if he should answer the first question in a similar manner, that he would then render himself inelligible to membership.

Our contention is that the second, third, and fourth questions are not exceptions, but that each candidate is expected to give an affirmative answer. If any had doubts or difficulties in reference to the subject, an effort was made in the conferences (especially those held by Wesley) to remove their troubles by a thorough canvass of the subject.

Let us look at these questions for a moment. What meaning can the 2nd, "Are you going on to perfection," have? No other than that they were to seek after the second blessing as taught by Wesley.

It was not for conversion, but for something that followed after that grace.

Neither is it to be a mere striving *to-ward* an impossible ideal, as the next question, "Do you expect to be made perfect in love in *this life,*" implies.

Wesley's definition of perfection, as "perfect love," or loving God with all the heart and neighbor as ourself, makes it clear that it is a blessing to be obtained in this life.

The next question, "Are you earnestly striving

(old discipline says *"groaning"*) after it," indicates that they are to seek it with all their heart, and "expect it every moment," as Wesley says.

It is clear from these questions, that all who already "have faith in Christ" are expected to seek and obtain this great blessing.

This obligation is just as binding today as at any time in the history of the church. If God, at that time, or any time, gave a *"second blessing"* to regenerate men, which more thoroughly equipped them for work in His vineyard, has He not the same for all to-day? Or has He been respecter of persons? His grace and fulness of salvation is just as available today as then, and if we do not obtain the baptism with the Holy Spirit for cleansing and for service, shall we not be responsible for the good we might have done and did not and could not do, because we lacked this equipment? "Let us fear, lest a promise being left us of entering into his rest, any of you should seem to come short of it."

The M. E. Discipline upholds the teaching of a *second blessing,* and true interpretation cannot arrive at any other conclusion, for it must be interpreted in the light of the teaching of John Wesley upon this subject; and we have already seen that he teaches a *"second blessing,"* and also calls it by that name.

CHAPTER VI.

The General Conference of 1852 authorized the publication of a series of catechisms known as Numbers 1, 2 and 3, thus indirectly making them a standard of doctrine.

I quote from No. 3.

Ques. "54. What fruits doth this faith produce? Ans. Justification, regeneration, sanctification."

Ques. "55. What is justification? Ans. Justification is that act of God's free grace in which He pardons our sins and accepts us as righteous in His sight for the sake of Christ."

Ques. "56. What is regeneration? Ans. It is the new birth of the soul in the image of Christ, whereby we become the children of God."

Ques. "57. What is sanctification? Ans. Sanctification is that act of divine grace whereby we are made holy."

Ques. "58. May every believer be wholly sanctified in this life? Ans. Yes; God's command is, 'Be ye holy, for I am holy'; and His promise is, that 'if we confess our sins' He will 'cleanse us from all unrighteousness.' "

On page 37, under a summary of these questions, we find this statement: *"It is the privilege of every believer to be wholly sanctified, and to love God with all his heart in the present life."*

None can intelligently read these questions and answers without perceiving that a difference is made between *regeneration* and *sanctification*— that one follows the other, or to be more definite, that sanctification is subsequent to regeneration— thus a *second* work of grace or blessing.

On page 38, at the bottom of the page, we have a definition of conversion. "A. *Conversion,* which, implying a complete renewal of heart and life, comprehends justification, regeneration and adoption."

You notice it does not include entire sanctification. The next question is:

"Q. When is sanctification begun? A. In regeneration, by which we receive power to grow in grace and in the knowledge of Christ," etc.

"Q. What is entire sanctification? A. The state of being *entirely* cleansed from sin, so as to love

God with all our heart, and mind, and soul, and strength, and our neighbor as ourselves."

Nothing is clearer from the above than that *entire* sanctification is subsequent to regeneration, thus a *second* blessing "properly socalled."

I will quote again from what is called *"The Larger Catechism."* This has been placed by the Bishops in the course of study for traveling preachers, and is therefore an authority in the church. Every preacher must study this, and pass examination thereon before he will be admitted on trial in our Annual Conference. Beginning on page 122, the Witness of the Spirit, Justification, Regeneration and Conversion are discussed, and immediately following on page 124, under question 294, we have this:

"Q. 294. What is sanctification? A. Sanctification is that act of Divine grace, whereby we are made holy."

"Q. 295. Can and ought a child of God to be cleansed from all sin in this life? A. Yes; the divine command is, 'Be ye holy, for I am holy,' with the promise that 'if we confess our sins, He will cleanse us from all unrighteousness.'"

Here again sanctification is something that is

to be obtained *after* regeneration, for it is the *child of God* that is to receive it.

Under question 296 is a definition of Christian perfection, which we desire to include in this chapter.

"296. In what does Christian perfection consist? A. Neither in knowledge nor in the full restoration of those powers of body and mind which Adam possessed before the fall; but in loving God with all our heart, with all our soul, with all our mind, and with all our strength, and our neighbor as ourself."

Surely the catechism sustains our position, that *entire sanctification* as a second work of grace is a doctrine of the M. E. Church.

We will quote from *"One Thousand Questions and Answers Concerning the Methodist Episcopal Church,"* by Henry Wheeler, D. D. Although this is not a catechism proper, yet it is of the same nature. Henry A. Buttz, of Drew Theological Seminary, in the introduction to this book, unhesitatingly recommends it to preachers and people. It is also in the course of study for traveling preachers, and thus may be considered an authority in Methodism.

In the chapter on "Doctrines" we find these questions:

"506. What is sanctification? A. It is that act of divine grace whereby we are made holy, wrought in the soul by the Holy Spirit AFTER RE-GENERATION, *and is the completion of the work begun in regeneration.* By this the true believer is enabled to love God with all his heart, and his neighbor as himself."

"507. Are these high attainments in the divine life for all men? It is the privilege of *every believer* to be wholly sanctified, and to love God with all his heart in the present life."

No comment is necessary. Our position is abundantly sustained by the catechism.

CHAPTER VII.

PROOF FROM THEOLOGIES.

Dr. Adam Clarke, the "prince of commentators," says: "If the Methodists give up preaching entire sanctification, they will soon lose their glory." Then speaking of *fitness* for heaven, he says: "This fitness, then, to appear before God, and thorough preparation for eternal glory, *is what I plead for, pray for, and heartily recommend* to all true believers, under the name of *Christian perfection.*" Theology, p. 201.

Again he says: "What, then, is this complete sanctification? It is the cleansing of the blood, that has not been cleansed; it *is washing the soul of a true believer from the remains of sin.*"—Theology, p. 206.

Once more from Clarke: "We are come to God for an *instantaneous* and *complete purification* from all sin, as for *instantaneous pardon.* In no part of the Scriptures are we directed to seek the remission of sins *seriatum*—one now and another

then, and so on. *Neither in any part are we di-*
rected to seek holiness by gradation. Neither a
gradation pardon nor a gradation PURIFICATION
exists in the Bible." Theology, p. 208.

Entire sanctification is a *second* work instantaneously obtained, according to Clarke.

Watson's Theological Institutes have been a
standard of Methodism, and are given in an
abridged form in Wakefield's. We quote from
him:

"We have already spoken of justification, adoption, regeneration, and the witness of the Holy
Spirit, and we proceed to another as distinctly
marked, and as graciously promised in the Holy
Scriptures: this is the ENTIRE SANCTIFICATION or
the perfected HOLINESS of believers; * * *"

"That a distinction exists between *a regenerate*
state and a *state of entire and perfect holiness*
will be generally allowed. Regeneration we have
seen, is concomitant with justification; but the
apostles, in addressing the body of believers in the
churches to whom they wrote their epistles, set before them, both in the prayers they offer in their
behalf, and in the exhortations they administer, a
still higher degree of deliverance from sin, as well

as a higher growth in Christian virtues." (Italics and capitals his own.)—*Theological Institutes,* Vol. II, p. 450.

He argues the subject at length, showing it to be a *second* attainment.

Our next witness is Dr. Raymond. He says: "Entire sanctification is not usually, if ever, contemporary with regeneration. Regeneration is, in most cases of Christian experience, if not in all, initial sanctification—not complete, perfect renewal. *The regenerated person is not at the moment of his regeneration, wholly sanctified."*— *Systematic Theology,* Vol. 2, p. 375.

As to its obtainment, he says: "It is obvious that the work of complete sanctification is both progressive and instantaneous,—progressive as to the acquisition of knowledge and ability to know, and *instantaneous* as to the *appropriation of the blessing* comprehended."—Vol. 2, p. 393.

Dr. Raymond is evidently on the side of the *second blessing* teaching.

We will now take some extracts from Dr. Pope. In Vol. 3 of his Theology, on page 45, under the heading, *"Purification from Sin, or Entire Sanctification,"* he says: "The virtue of the atonement,

administered by the Holy Spirit, is set forth in
Scripture as effecting entire destruction of sin.
This is everywhere declared to be the design of
redemption; and it is promised to the *believer* as
his necessary preparation for the future life. The
entire removal of sin from the nature is nowhere
connected with any other means than the Word
of God received in faith and proved in experience."

He gives this testimony to the Wesleys: "The
doctrine of Christian Perfection which the Wesleys taught was very early embraced, and in its
main elements was consistently maintained
throughout their career." * * *

"From the very beginning it (Methodism) had
this burden committed to it; the clear views of
its founders as to the acceptance of the believer,
and his assurance of acceptance, were connected
from the very outset with clear views as to the
privilege of being filled with the love of God and
delivered from indwelling sin, and attaining as a
result, a state of evangelical perfection."—Vol. 3,
p 88.

In the last part of this he means to say, that
the one who has the assurance of his acceptance

with God, has the privilege of being delivered from inbred sin and filled with the love of God.

"The Methodist doctrine is the only one that has consistently and boldly maintained the possibility of the destruction of the carnal mind, or the inbred sin of our fallen nature."

*   *   *   *

"The combination of the two elements, the negative annihilation of the principle of sin, and the positive effusion of perfect love, is, it may be said, peculiar to Methodist theology as such." Vol. 3, p. 97.

"Finally, the doctrine which runs through the works and whole career of the Wesleys is marked by its reasonableness and moderation, as well as its sublimity."—Vol. 3, p. 99.

It seems that Dr. Pope was for a time prejudiced against the use of the phrase *"second blessing,"* but was led finally to give it up and accept it as a proper term. We quote a part of an address given by him at the British Conference:

"I have sometimes very delicately scrupled at this, that, and the other expression, and I have wondered whether it is right to speak of a *'second blessing'*; and I have taken a text in which our

Savior takes a blind man and partially restores him his sight, and then holding the man up before us for a little while, that we may study his state, which is a great advance upon what it was, that we may watch him in this state of struggle between sin and the flesh, He touches him again, and he sees every man clearly. *In the face of that text, and in the face of the experience of multitudes of our fathers; in the face of the testimonies of multitudes now living, and in the face of the deep instinct, the hope and desire of my own unworthy heart, I* WILL NEVER AGAIN WRITE AGAINST THE PHRASEOLOGY REFERRED TO."

We commend this candid statement from this profound man to all who have similar prejudices.

We next quote from "Binney's Theological Compend." This book is in the course of study for local preachers, and is therefore considered an authority in the church.

"Holiness begins when the principle of purity, namely, love to God, is shed abroad in the heart in the new birth. But entire sanctification is that act of the Holy Ghost whereby the *justified* soul is made holy. This *instantaneous* work of the Sanctifier is usually preceded and followed by a gradual growth in grace."—Page 128.

"*Purity* is to be distinguished from *maturity.* When inbred sin is destroyed, there can be no increase in purity, but there may be an eternal increase in love, and in all the fruits of the Spirit. *Sanctification is not the same with justification. Justification* is a change of our *state* from guilt to pardon; *sanctification* is a change of our *nature* from sin to holiness. It sustains to regeneration the relation of a whole to a part." Page 129.

The doctrine of an instantaneous "*second blessing*" is unmistakably sustained by this book.

Our next witness will be Dr. Miley, of Drew Theological Seminary. His Systematic Theology, embracing two volumes, is in the course of study for traveling preachers. We quote from Vol. II.

"The doctrine of an incompleteness of the work of regeneration underlies that of entire sanctification, *particularly in its Wesleyan form.* Without such incompleteness, there could be no place for the definite second-blessing view. That somewhat of depravity remains in the regenerate, or that regeneration does not bring to completeness the inner spiritual life, is a widely accepted doctrine.

Indeed, exceptions are so few that the doctrine must be regarded as truly catholic. * * * Hence, there is a place for the doctrine of entire sanctification as an attainable blessing in the present life." Page 357.

"Underlying the definite second blessing view is the doctrine of a common incompleteness of the work of regeneration. Herein the soul is renewed, but not wholly; purified, but not thoroughly. Somewhat of depravity remains, which wars against the new spiritual life; not strong enough to bring that life into bondage to itself, yet strong enough to impose a burden upon the work of its maintainance. Such is the first part. The doctrine in the second part is that the regenerate shall come to the consciousness of this incompleteness, and to a deep sense of the need of a fullness of the spiritual life; that these experiences shall be analagous to those which preceded the attainment of regeneration, and be just as deep and thorough. The fullness of sanctification shall be instantly attained on the condition of faith, just as justification is attained; and there shall be a new experience of a great and gracious change, and just as consciously such as the experience of regeneration.

"*That Mr. Wesley held and taught such views there can be no doubt;* though we think it would be a wrong to him to say that he allowed no instances of entire sanctification except in this definite mode. We see no perplexity for faith in the possibility of such an instant subjective purification.*"

He declares that this instantaneous purification does not forbid some preparation for its attainment, and says: "However, this process of preparation need not be chronologically long. No assumption of such a necessity could be true to the soteriology of the Scriptures. Let it be recalled that the question here is, not the *maturity* of the Christian life, but the *purification* of the nature. For the attainment of the former there must be growth, and growth requires time. But, while the subjective purification *may* be progressively wrought, *it is not subject to the law of growth; and it is so thoroughly and solely the work of God that it may be quickly wrought.* Neither is there any necessity that the mental process of preparation shall be chronologically a long one. Here, as in many other spheres, the mental movement may be rapid. It is often so in conversion. *In many* instances the whole mental process has been crowded into one hour or even less time. Even heathen have been saved, born of the Spirit through faith in Christ, under the first sermon they ever heard. But there is as really a necessary process of preparation for regeneration as for entire sanctification; and such preparation need require no more time in the latter case than in the former."

* * * *

"*Mr. Wesley held strongly the view of an instant subjective sanctification; and we fully agree with him, not only in its possibility, but also in its frequent actuality.*"

* * * *

"The privilege of entire sanctification is at once so thoroughly scriptural and Wesleyan that from it there is among us only the rarest dissent. Yet not a few hesitate respecting the sharply defined *second blessing view*. WE DO NOT SHARE THIS HESITATION, *so far as that view represents a possible mode of entire sanctification,* though we object to any insistance that such is the only possible mode." Pages 368-371.

Dr. Miley admits:—

1. That sin remains in the regenerate.

2. That it is removed in entire sanctification as a *second blessing.*

3. That this blessing may be received as instantly as was justification.

4. He maintains that it is scriptural and Wesleyan, but would not confine it to only one mode.

While Mr. Wesley did not deny the *possibility* of a gradual work, yet his testimony is strongly on the side of the instantaneous. It may not be out of place here to let him speak for himself. In a sermon written only a short time before his death he gives a review of the great holiness revival that began in 1759. He speaks of the large numbers who professed sanctification in England and Ireland, from that time to the present, and how he examined the most of them himself, and adds: "And everyone of these (after the most care inquiry, *I have not found one exception, either in Great Britain or Ireland*) has declared that his deliverance from sin was *instantaneous;* that the change was wrought in a moment. Had half of these, or one-third, or one in twenty, declared it was *gradually* wrought in *them,* I should have believed this, with regard to *them,* and thought that

some were gradually sanctified and some instantaneously. *But as I have not found, in so long a*
space of time, a single person speaking thus; as
all who believe they are sanctified, declare with one
voice, that the change was wrought in a moment, I
CANNOT BUT BELIEVE THAT SANCTIFICATION IS
COMMONLY, IF NOT ALWAYS, AN INSTANTANEOUS
WORK." Ser., Vol. II., p. 223.

I would like to ask if any one has ever found
one witness to this grace who had been *gradually*
sanctified. None deny a gradual approach to
and preparation for either regeneration or sanctification; but this gradual approach is not either
the one or the other of these blessings. We do
deny, with Dr. Miley above, the necessity of a long
interval of time between regeneration and entire
sanctification, and believe, as Wesley says, that "it
is COMMONLY, IF NOT ALWAYS INSTANTANEOUS."

No matter how long the preparation; no matter how near the soul has approximated *to* entire
sanctification, it cannot say it is done until that
last moment when, instantly, by the breath of God,
sin is destroyed. Then, and only then, will or
can the Spirit witness to purity of heart; then,

and only then, can one say, "I am clean from my sin."

It appears, then, in the last analysis that *entire* sanctification is always instantaneous. But this point is rather beside our purpose.

One of the most profound thinkers and theologians of the M. E. Church is Bishop R. S. Foster. A short time ago he said that his book, *"Christian Purity,"* "teaches plainly all the views I hold on this subject." We will take some extracts from it.

In chapter II, he sets forth the several different theories which are held. We will give a summary of the two main theories:

1. All who are regenerated are entirely sanctified. Nothing else is necessary or possible.

2. Regeneration is not entire sanctification, but depravity remains.

This again divides into four classes:

(a) Those who hold that entire sanctification takes place in the article of death.

(b) There is a gradual growth until all the graces are fully ripened and the person immediately dies.

(c) May come to maturity by a gradual growth and continue to live.

(d) May obtain at any time after regeneration an instantaneous deliverance from the remains of sin and live a life of holiness..

In the first paragraph of Chapter III, he identifies himself with the last named theory above, and says:

"1. The following pages will be given to a defense of the ultimate theory in the above category. In our deepest conviction, it contains the truth—*nothing but the truth*—THE ENTIRE TRUTH; a truth the most momentous, and also the most glorious in the universe. 'Man may be holy and live! Man *must* be holy, or he *cannot* live, in the highest sense!' " (Italics and capitals his own.)

I refer all to his book named above for his arguments sustaining the doctrine of a *"second blessing,* properly socalled."

The theologians and theologies of Methodism abundantly sustain our position.

CHAPTER VIII.

EPISCOPAL DELIVERANCES.

The General Conference of the M. E. Church, which meets once in four years, is the law-making body of the church. Its deliverances are to be looked upon as authoritative. From time to time, this body has directly or indirectly defined entire sanctification and emphasized its great importance.

In 1824, the Bishops said in their pastoral address, "Never was there a period more momentously interesting to our church than the present. Do we as preachers feel the same child-like spirit which so eminently marked our first ministers? Do we come to the people in the fullness of the blessing of the gospel of peace? It is not enough to preach the gospel truth, but we must preach a full gospel from a full heart and preach it, too, in demonstration of the Spirit and with power. And above all, do we insist on the present witness of the Spirit and entire sanctification through faith

in Christ? *Are we striving by faith and obedi-*
ence to elevate our hearts and lives to the stand-
ard of gospel holiness; or are we wishing to have
the standard lowered to our unsanctified natures?
In short, are we contented to have the doctrine
of Christian holiness an article of our creed only,
without becoming experimentally and practically
acquainted with it? Or are we pressing after it
as the prize of our high calling in Christ Jesus?
"IF METHODISTS GIVE UP THE DOC-
TRINE OF ENTIRE SANCTIFICATION, OR
SUFFER IT TO BECOME A DEAD LETTER,
WE ARE A FALLEN POPLE. (Capitals ours.)
It is this that lays the ax at the root of the Anti-
nomian tree in all its forms and degrees of
growth; it is this that inflames and diffuses life,
rouses to action, prompts to perseverance, and
urges the soul forward to every holy exercise and
every useful work. IF THE METHODISTS
LOSE SIGHT OF THE DOCTRINE THEY
WILL FALL BY THEIR OWN WEIGHT,
THEIR SUCCESS IN GAINING NUMBERS
WILL BE THE CAUSE OF THEIR DISSOLU-
TION. HOLINESS IS THE MAIN CORD
THAT BINDS US TOGETHER. RELAX

THIS, AND YOU LOOSEN THE WHOLE
SYSTEM." (Capitals ours.)

If there is a decline in Methodism, may not the
reason be found in the fact of having given up
the doctrine, or at least in allowing it to become a
dead letter? Yea, more in directly antagonizing
it?

In the Pastoral Address of 1832 we find this
definition and exhortation:

"When we speak of holiness, we mean that state
in which God is loved with all the heart, and
served with all the powers. This, as Methodists,
we have said, *is the privilege of the Christian* IN
THIS LIFE; *and we have further said that the
privilege may be secured* INSTANTANEOUSLY *by an
act of faith,* AS JUSTIFICATION WAS. * * * Only
let all who have been born of the Spirit and have
tasted the good word of God, *seek with the same
ardor to be made perfect in love as they sought
for the pardon of their sins,* and soon will our
class-meetings and love-feasts be cheered by the
relation of experience of this high character, as
they now are with those which tell of justification
and the new birth. And when this shall come to
be the case, we may expect a corresponding in-

crease in the amount of our Christian enjoyment, and in the force of religious influence we shall exert over others." *Bang's History M. E. Church,* Vol. IV., p. 81.

Here is a clear declaration by the highest body of Methodism, that holiness is a work of grace *subsequent* to regeneration; and also of the importance of its possession and profession.

We quote again from the pastoral address of 1840:

"The doctrine of entire sanctification constitutes a leading feature of original Methodism. But let us not suppose it enough to have this doctrine in our standards: let us labor to have the *experience* and the *power* of it in our *hearts.* Be assured, brethren, *that if our influence and usefulness, as a religious community depend upon one thing more than another, it is upon our carrying out the great doctrine of sanctification in our life and conversation.* WHEN WE FAIL TO DO THIS, THEN SHALL WE LOSE OUR PRE-EMINENCE, AND THE HALO OF GLORY WHICH SURROUNDED THE HEADS AND LIT UP THE PATH OF OUR SAINTED FATHERS, WILL HAVE DEPARTED FROM THEIR UNWORTHY SONS." Bangs, Vol. 4, p. 421.

The heart grows sick as we read the latter part of this prophecy, *for we see it has come to pass!* ICHABOD! *O, Methodism! thy glory is departed.'*

The Bishops, in their address to the General Conference in 1896, made this clear statement as to the position of the M. E. Church: "As a church, we have taught, *from the beginning,* that believers have power to become the sons of God— be made partakers of the divine nature. *We have insisted on the glorious privilege and duty of all men becoming saints, of* IMMEDIATELY *being made perfect in love,* and of gradually ripening into Christian maturity in all faculties. This doctrine was never more definitely stated, clearly perceived, nor consistently lived by greater numbers than now." Note these facts:

1. They say it has been a doctrine of the church *from the beginning.*

2. It is a privilege and also duty to become a saint, or be made perfect in love, and that *instantaneously.*

In the Episcopal address to the General Conference, which was held in 1900, we find these significant expressions: "Inasmuch as the permanence and growth of the Christian Church, and of any part of it, are inseparable from fidelity to the truth as it is in Jesus, we rejoice to report our belief *that the theological convictions and teachings of our church are, in the main unchanged;* that through its entire extent, at home and abroad, the essential Christian verities, AS RECEIVED FROM OUR FATHERS, and by which we have hitherto ministered successfully to the kingdom of God, are firmly held and positively proclaimed."

From the re-statement of the creed that follows, we quote again:

"We believe that faith in Christ, the self-surrender of the soul to His government and grace, is the one condition upon which man is reconciled to God, is born again, becomes partaker of the divine nature, *and attains sanctification through the Spirit.*"

Continuing, they speak of the work yet to be done in bringing the world to Christ, and emphasize the fact that we should not be content with past, nor even present attainments. "How can we be content while there sounds in our ears the word which fixes duty and assures victory? 'All power is given unto me in heaven and in earth. Lo! I am with you always, even to the end of the world.'

While Pentecost shines upon us from afar, *the ever luminous instance of what God intended His Church to receive, to became and to achieve;* while great, auspicious promises *summon us to perfect personal holiness* and triumph like those of the great apostle?"

In the Bishop's address to the General Conference held at Los Angeles in 1904 we find the following:—

* * * "John Wesley must have ascertained and built upon *fundamental and imperishable truths,* else the world would never have heard of Methodism. Among those truths which he lifted out of the dust of ages were at least these: the deep guilt of sin; the equal redemption all men by the vicarious atonement; the absolut freedom of the human will; the entire practicabil. of salvation now for any sinner: THE ATTAIN. ILITY OF PERFECT CLEANSING AND PERFECT LOVE IN THIS LIFES etc," *Daily Advocate.* p 36.

(Italics and capitals ours.)

This doctrine is looked upon as a *"fundamental and imperishable truth,"* and from their statement on page 35 of Daily Advocate—"Salvation *going on to* perfect cleansing and perfect love,"—

it is evident that they believe it to be received af-
tr conversion and thus a "Second attainment" or
"blessing."

Although these statements of the Bishops are
not as *definite* as some others given, yet, because of
their reference to the past—to the teachings received from the fathers—they become competent
witnesses to the doctrine of entire sanctification as
a *second* attainment. Their inferential and cir-
cumstantial evidence is undeniable. They sustain our position.

We will give one quotation from the address of
the Bishops of the M. E. Church, South, made to
their General Conference in 1894: "The privilege
of *believers* to attain unto a state of entire sanctification or perfect love, and to abide therein, *is a
well known teaching of Methodism*. Witnesses to
this experience have never been wanting in the
church, though few in comparison with the whole
membership. Among them have been men and
women of beautiful consistency, and seraphic ardor, jewels of the church. Let the doctrine still
be proclaimed and the experience still be testified."

We need no further witnesses to prove our position that entire sanctification as a SECOND BLESS-
ING *is a doctrine of Methodism, North and South.*

CHAPTER IX.

CHIPS.

Under this heading we will insert a few individual statements. These are strong proofs of our position. The first will be taken from McClintock and Strong's Cyclopedia:

"Methodism teaches, also, that it is the privilege of *believers in this life* to reach that maturity of grace, and that conformity to the divine, which cleanses the heart from sin and fills it with love to God and man—the being filled, as Paul phrases it, with all the fulness of God. This they call Christian perfection, a state which they declare to be attainable through *faith* in Christ." *Vol. VI., Art. Methodism.*

On January 27, 1767, Wesley wrote these "Brief Thoughts on Christian Perfection":

"1. By perfection I mean the humble, gentle, patient love of God and our neighbor, ruling our tempers, words and actions.

"2. As to the manner. I believe this perfection

is *always* wrought in the soul by a simple act of faith; consequently in one instant. But I believe a gradual work, both preceding and following that instant.

"3. As to the time. I believe this instant generally is the instant of death, the moment before the soul leaves the body. *But I believe it may be ten, twenty, or forty years before.*

"I believe it is usually many years after justification; but that it may be within five years or five months after it; I know no conclusive argument to the contrary.

"If it must be many years after justification, I would be glad to know how many. What length of time will sanction it? And how many days, or months, or even years, can any one allow to be between perfection and death? How far from justification must it be; and how near to death?" —*Works, Vol. VI., page* 531.

We will give two more extracts from Wesley as to a second work and to its instantaneousness.

"You may obtain a 'growing' victory 'over' sin from the moment you are justified. 'But this is not enough'; the 'body of sin,' the 'carnal mind,' *must be 'destroyed';* the old man must be slain, or we cannot put on the new man, which is created after God (or which is the image of God) in righteousness and true holiness; *and this is 'done in a moment.' To talk of this work as being gradual would be nonsense, as much as if we talked of gradual justification."— H. A. Rogers' Journal, page* 174.

" 'But does God work this great work in the soul gradually or instantaneously?' Perhaps it may be gradually wrought in some; *I mean in this sense: they do not advert to the particular moment wherein sin ceases.* But it is *infinitely desirable,* were it the will of God, that it should be done instantaneously; that the Lord should *destroy* sin 'by the breath of his mouth' in a moment, in the twinkling of an eye. And this he generally does; a plain fact, of which there is evidence enough to satisfy any unprejudiced person." —*Sermon, Scripture Way of Salvation.*

These facts are found in the above:

1.   After justification there may be a 'growing' victory over sin.

2.   But the "carnal mind" must *be destroyed*— it cannot be grown out.

3.   This is done in a moment.

4. He means by a gradual work, that they are not able to tell precisely *when* the blessing was received, although they are now conscious of possessing it.

5. It is *"infinitely desirable"* that it be *instantaneous;* that is, that they should be able to tell the time when the work. was done.

In the *Central Christian Advocate* for Feb. 12, 1902 was an article on "Methodist Doctrine," by H. C. Sheldon, S.T.D., Professor of Dogmatic Theology in Boston University. He speaks of Wesley's doctrine of Christian perfection thus:

"It was manifestly his conviction that the work of grace which takes place in regeneration *may be followed* by a great consummating work worthy to be called *entire* sanctification; that entire sanctification, whatever intellectual and bodily defects it may fail to heal, not merely gives a normal direction to the will, but reaches back into the emotive nature, the sphere of impulses, desires and affections, and profoundly renovates this background of the volitional life. Supposing the term 'inbred sin' to cover all perverse tendencies of the emotive nature, we may say that Wesley taught that entire sanctification includes the *elim-*

ination of inbred sin. That this was his teaching, is indicated by the broad antithesis which he made between regeneration and entire sanctification; by his contention that the transformation which Protestant thnking of his time commonly associated with the article of death, can be substantially realized at an earlier point in the career of an individual; and by unequivocal expressions in the hymns of his brother Charles, who may be presumed to share his way of thinking."

In the *Christian Witness,* of Chicago, for Feb. 19, 1903, in the "Question Box," Dr. Steele gives this answer to question 1245, "Are there in the original any important various readings in the Lord's Prayer":

"Ans. In Westcott and Hort's Greek Testament, also in Alford's, there is noted a very interesting rejected text. Instead of the clause, 'Thy kingdom come,' some copyist in the first half of the second century has this sentence in Luke 11:2, 'Let thy Holy Spirit come upon us and cleanse.' This may have been at first a marginal comment which Marcion (A. D. 139-180) purposely interpolated, or some copyist copied into the text as explanatory of the kingdom and afterwards some other copyist substituted for the prayer for its coming. *It is valuable as a proof that a prominent writer immediately after the days of the apostles identified the kingdom of God on the earth with the cleansing efficacy of the Holy Spirit, and that the disciples of Christ may be genuine believers before they are entirely sanctified—a blessing for which they should pray."*

The General Conference minutes for 1807 has a somewhat lengthy obituary of Bishop Whatcoat. We quote a short extract:

"Richard Whatcoat was born in 1736, at Quinton, Gloucestershire, Old England, became a hearer of the Methodists at 21 years of age. Converted Sept. 3, 1758. *Sanctified* March 28, 1761. * * * Died in Dover, Del., July 5, 1806."

In a letter to his brother Charles, Wesley says: "I still think, to disbelieve all the professors, amounts to a denial of the thing. For if there be no living witnesses of what we have preached for twenty years, I cannot, dare not, preach it any longer. The whole comes to one point: *Is there, or is there not, any instantaneous sanctification be-tween justification and death? I* SAY YES; you ('often seem' to) say, No. What arguments brought you to think so? Perhaps they may con-vince me, too."—Works, Vol. VI., p. 669.

In a letter to a Mrs. A. F., Oct. 12, 1764, Wesley writes:

"That great truth, 'that we are saved by faith,' will never be worn out; and that sanctifying as well as justifying faith is the free gift of God. Now with God one day is as a thousand years. It plainly follows that the quantity of time is noth-ing to Him. * * * Consequently He can as well sanctify in a day *after* we are justified, as a hun-dred years. * * * Accordingly we see in fact, that some of the most unquestionable witnesses of sanc-tifying grace were sanctified within a few days after they were justified. I have seldom known so devoted a soul as S— H—, at Macclesfield, who was sanctified within nine days after she was con-vinced of sin." Vol. 7, p. 14.

Bishop R. S. Foster says: "The process of the work (of sanctification) is in this order: begin-ning with pardon, by which one aspect of sin, that is actual guilt, is wholly removed, and proceeding in regeneration, by which another kind of sin, that is depravity, is in part removed, terminating with entire sanctification, by which the remainder of the second kind, or depravity, is entirely removed." —*Christian Purity, p.* 121.

The difference between sin and depravity is thus given by J. A. Wood:

"1. Sin is 'the transgression of the law,' and involves moral action, either by voluntary *omission* or wilful *commission,* and always incurs guilt.

"2. Depravity is a *state* or *condition,* a defilement or perversity of spirit. It is developed in the soul, in inclinations to sin, or in sinward tendencies.

"3. Sin, strictly speaking, is voluntary, and involves responsible action, and is a thing to be *pardoned.*

"4. Depravity is *inborn,* inherited, and *inbred.* It is derived from fallen Adam, and is augmented by actual sin.

"5. All sin involves *guilt;* depravity does not, unless it be assented to, cherished, or its cure wilfully neglected.

"6. Depravity is one of the *results* of sin, and it may have somewhat of the nature of sin, in the sense of being a *disconformity* or *unlikeness* to God; and it is in this sense that 'all unrighteousness is sin.' Depravity lacks the voluntary element of sin, hence it is not a thing to be *pardoned*, like sin proper, but is to be removed from the soul by *cleansing* or purgation." *Perfect Love, p.* 42.

Bishop Foster says: "Sin committed, and depravity felt, are very different; the one is an action, the other *a state of the affections.* The regenerate believer is saved from the one, and he has grace to enable him to have the victory over the other; but *the disposition* itself, to some extent, remains under the control of a stronger, gracious power implanted, but still making resistance and indicating actual presence, and needing to be *entirely* sanctified."—*Christian Purity,* p. 111.

This chapter might be made much longer, but are there not enough facts in it to prove our proposition? Methodism does teach a second blessing, or work of grace.

CHAPTER X.

WITNESSES.

Out of a multitude of witnesses to entire sanctification as a second work of grace, we can give but
few.

Two witnesses to a matter of fact are sufficient
to establish a case before a civil court; but naturally the greater the number of reliable witnesses,
the greater weight their testimony will have in a
given case.

The method of the objector at present seems to
be to deny the ability of the common people to
judge their religious experience. They imply by
this, that they do not understand psychology, etc.,
and therefore are not competent witnesses as to
their conscious states. If that is true, then they
must be excluded from testimony in the civil
courts, as they would be no more competent in a
case of this kind than in the other. Such a conclusion is absurd, and we unhesitatingly deny the
truth of their position.

All through the centuries since Christ, men have been saying to the world, "I *know* Him whom I have believed." Paul, the Apostle, declared that God had revealed His Son in him (Gal. 1:15,16), and that God has given unto us His Spirit, "that we might *know* the things that are freely given to us by God." (1 Cor. 2:12.) Again he says, "For our glory is this, the testimony of our conscience, that in *holiness* and sincerity of God, not in fleshly wisdom, but in the grace of God, we behaved ourselves in the world, etc." (2 Cor. 1:12, R. V.)

Of course if Paul had had the privilege of sitting at the feet of some of the modern psychologists, he would not have expressed himself so freely, but being ignorant of the discoveries of these modern wise men, he was so unscientific as to believe that the Spirit could witness not only to sonship with God (Rom. 8:15, 16), but also to holiness of heart (1 Cor. 2:12; 2 Cor. 1:12).

We are unscientific enough to believe with Paul, that God has given us His Spirit that we may KNOW the things—not one, but *all* that He shall do for us in the way of our soul's relation to Him.

No sinner need to ask the "new" psychology whether his consciousness of guilt and condemnation is the result of bad digestion or a sluggish liver; he *knows* that he is a violator of God's holy law, and that His displeasure rests upon him. So the one who has turned from his sins and believed on the Lord Jesus Christ, *knows* that his sins are forgiven and God is now reconciled, "because he hath the witness in himself."

Surely the Spirit can witness to one state as easily as the other. Of this there can be no doubt.

He can witness to guilt—or convince of sin, and to its removal; to uncleanness and to holiness. If we exclude either, all must go. There is absolutely no reason why He cannot and should not witness to one of these conscious states as well as the other.

But we cannot follow this subject further. We *do* receive the testimony of men in all things pertaining to our relation one with the other. If two or three testify as to a matter of fact or experience, we are bound to receive their witness. We propose to produce a sufficient number of *competent* witnesses to establish the fact of a *"second blessing,"* or work of grace. This doctrine is not new, and God has had His witnesses all through the centuries.

In the eighth chapter of Acts an account is given of a revival which was held by Philip. The whole city was stirred. Many believed, unclean spirits were cast out, and other great signs were wrought, "and there was great joy in that city." Philip had a baptizing and took a large number of both men and women into the church. No one dare say these were not converted as we use that term. But notice, as soon as the news reached the apostles at Jerusalem, they sent Peter and John down to teach them about the second blessing, and they prayed for them, laid their hands upon them, and they received the Holy Ghost. *Here is a clear case of a* SECOND *crisis in the experience of these people that cannot be argued away.* Others might be given from the New Testament, but this is sufficient.

Ignatius, who lived and wrote between A. D. 100 and 200, says: "Faith is the beginning, love the end; and both being joined in one are of God. All other things pertaining to perfect holiness follow." Again he says, "I thank Thee, O, Lord, that Thou hast vouchsafed to honor me with a *perfect love* towards Thee."

Macarius lived about 325 A. D. He seems to have been a clear teacher of a further work of grace. In his Homilies he writes: "One that is rich in grace, at all times, by night and by day, continues in a perfect state, free and pure, ever captivated with love, and ever elevated to God." "In like manner Christians, though outwardly tempted, yet inwardly they are filled with the Divine nature, and so nothing injured. *These degrees, if any man attain to, he is come to the perfect love of Christ, and to the fulness of the Godhead."*

"What, then, is that perfect will of God to which the apostle calls and exhorts every one of us to attain? *It is the perfect purity from sin, freedom from shameful passions, and the assumption of perfect virtue;* THAT IS THE PURIFICATION OF THE HEART BY THE PLENARY AND EXPERIMENTAL COMMUNION OF THE PERFECT DIVINE SPIRIT. To those who say that it is impossible to attain to perfection and the final and complete subjugation of the passions, or to acquire a full participation of the good Spirit, we must oppose the testimony of the divine Scriptures, and prove to them that they are ignorant and speak both falsely and presumptously."

Nothing is more clear than that here is set forth

an attainment beyond the experience of those who are merely converted—that is a purification of the heart and the fulness of the divine Spirit as a subsequent attainment, or *"second blessing."* This is sufficient to show that the teaching is not a new one, but comes to us from the time of the Master himself. He took a blind man, touched his eyes, and asked if he saw. And he said, "I see men as trees, walking." Jesus touched his eyes the *second* time, and he saw every man clearly. (Mark 8: 23-25.) Jesus said of His disciples that they had kept God's word (John 17:6), that the world hated them because they were not of the world, EVEN AS HE was not of the world, and yet He prays that they should be sanctified. (John 17: 14, 17.)

We will omit a long period of time and come to George Fox, the founder of the Quaker Church. He is a clear witness to a *second* work of grace. He says: "I knew Jesus, and He was very precious to my soul; but I found something within me that would not keep sweet, and patient, and kind. I did what I could to keep it down, but it was there; I besought Jesus to do something for me, and when I gave Him my will He came to my heart and took out all that would not be sweet, all that would not be kind, all that would not be patient, and then He shut the door."

We come now to John Wesley, the founder of Methodism. We frequently see his testimony to conversion, but seldom anything more than this. We quote from his Journal of May 24, 1738: "In the evening I went very unwillingly to a society in Aldersgate street, where one was reading Luther's preface to the Epistle to th Romans. About a quarter before nine, while he was describing the change which God works in the heart through faith in Christ, I felt my heart strangely warmed. I felt I did trust in Christ,—Christ alone for salvation; and an assurance was given me, that He had taken away my sins, even mine, and saved me from the law of sin and death. I began to pray with all my might for those who had in a more especial manner despitefully used me and persecuted me. I then testified openly to all there, what I now first felt in my heart."

The next day he says: "The moment I awakened, Jesus Master was in my heart and in my mouth, and I found all my strength lay in keeping my eye fixed upon him, and my soul waiting on him continually."

No comment upon this is needed. This is admitted by all to be an account of his conversion. But why have they not gone further and given his other most remarkable experience, which came about six years later? Any one reading his Journals immediately following the above experience will find him recording spiritual conflicts. He finally concluded to visit the Moravians in Germany and see if he could not receive help for his distracted soul. While there he says he enjoyed the blessing of hearing Christian David preach at four different times, and every time he chose the very subject Wesley would have desired had he spoken to him before. Thrice he described the state of those who are 'weak in faith,' who are *"justified, but have not yet a new, clean heart."* Another sermon treated of the state of the apostles before the day of Pentecost—that these men were "clean" and had "faith," but not in the *"full* sense did they have new hearts."

He gives the testimony of quite a number, who declare that they received another "blessing" AF-TER *they had been justified.*

He returns to England. Success crowns his ministry. From time to time he records his spiritual experience in such words as these: "In the evening our souls were so filled with the spirit of prayer and thanksgiving, that I could scarce tell how to expound." Vol. 3, p. 200. "But my heart was so enlarged, I knew not how to give over, so that we continued three hours." Vol. 3, p. 292. "The dread of God fell upon us while I was speaking, so that I could hardly utter a word; but most of all in prayer, wherein I was so carried out, as scarce ever before in my life." Vol. 3, p. 292.

Other extracts of this kind might be given; but we will pass on.

During this time he seemed to be troubled still with spiritual conflicts; but his full Pentecost is near at hand.

On December 23, 1744, he writes in his Journal: "I was unusually lifeless and heavy, till the love-feast in the evening; when, just as I was constraining myself to speak, I was stopped whether I would or no, for the blood gushed out of both my nostrils, so that I could not add another word; but in a few minutes it stayed, and all our hearts and mouths were opened to praise God. Yet the next day I was again as a dead man; *but in the evening, while I was reading prayers at Snows-field, I found such light and strength as I never remember to have had before.* I saw every thought, as well as action or word, just as it was rising in my heart; and whether it was right before God, or tainted with pride or selfishness. *I never knew before* (I mean not as at this time) what it was 'to be still before God.'"

On Tuesday, the 25th, he says: "I waked, by the grace of God, in the same spirit; and about eight, being with two or three that believed in Jesus, I felt such an awe and tender sense of the presence of God, *as greatly confirmed me therein;* so that God was before me all the day long. I sought and found him in every place; and could truly say, when I lay down at night, *'now I have lived a day.'*" Vol. 3, pp. 3421325.

Here is as clear a testimony to entire sanctification as he ever gave to conversion.

From this year onward as for as I have examined his writings, all evidence of inner spiritual conflicts disappear. He is now grounded and settled and holds steadily on his way regardless of men and devils.

In 1762, in a letter to Bell and Owen, he says, "You have over and over denied instantaneous sanctification to me; *but I have known* and taught it (and so has my brother, as our writings show) above these twenty years." Journal, Oct., 1762.

Again, he says, "Many years ago I saw that without holiness no man shall see the Lord. I began by following after it, and inciting all with whom I had any intercourse, to do the same. Ten years after God gave me a clearer view than I had before of the way how to attain it, namely, by faith in the Son of God. And immediately I declared to all, 'we are saved from sin, we are made holy by faith.' *This I testified in public,—in print,* and God confirmed it by a thousand witnesses." Vol. 7, p. 38, 1771.

Wesley was a living witness of the full salvation which he taught. There is no room to dispute it. John Fletcher, vicar of Madely; Hester Ann Rogers; William Bramwell; William Carvosso; Lady Maxwell, were also witnesses to, and advocates of the doctrine of a second work of grace.

Dr. Adam Clarke, the great commentator of the Wesleyan church and one of the most learned men of his day, obtained this blessing in the twenty-

second year of his age. He says; "I regarded
nothing, not even life itself, in comparison of having my heart *cleansed from all sin;* and began to
seek it with full purpose of heart." . . . . "Soon
after this, while earnestly wrestling with the Lord
in prayer, and endeavoring self-desperately to believe, *I found a change wrought in my soul,* which
I endeavored, through grace, to maintain amid the
grievous temptations and accusations of the subtle
foe."

He was led to seek this grace by a local preacher
who already enjoyed it.

Bishop Francis Asbury, the John Wesley of
America, is also a strong witness to this blessed
doctrine of entire sanctification as a subsequent
work of grace. In his journals from time to time
he speaks of his religious experience. He says, "I
was then about fifteen; and, young as I was, the
word of God soon made deep impressions on my
heart, which brought me to Jesus Christ, who graciously *justified* my guilty soul through faith in
his precious blood; and soon showed me the ex-
cellency and necessity of holiness. About sixteen
I experienced a marvelous display of the grace of

God, which some might think was full sanctification." Vol. 1. pp. 120-121, 1774.

In Vol. 2, p. 160, in a short sketch of nis life,
he speaks more definitely of this experience.
"Some time after I had obtained a clear witness of
my acceptance with God, the Lord showed me, in
the heat of youth and youthful blood, the *evil* of
my heart; for a short time I enjoyed, as I thought,
the pure and perfect love of God; but this happy
frame did not long continue, although at seasons
I was greatly blessed. . . . How I came to America, and the events which have happened since, my
journal will show."

Mr. Wesley said that it was more to *retain* this
blessing than to *obtain* it, and that many lost the
the witness a number of times before they became
established therein. This seems to have been the
case with Mr. Asbury.

In Vol. 1, of his Journals, page 305, he writes,
"I was inclined to believe, that the night before
the Lord had *re-sanctified* my soul. It afforded me
much comfort; and I was ready to conclude *it had
been so far many years past,* if I had maintained
and believed it. But I fear I have been too slack
in urging both myself and others diligently to

seek the experience of this great and blessed gift.
May the Lord help me from this time, to live free
from outward and inward sin, always maintaining
the spirit of ' the gospel in meekness, purity, and
love." 1779.

On page 308 of the same volume he says; "I
have not sufficiently enforced the doctrine of
Christian perfection. This will press *believers* forward, when everything else is found insufficient.
. . . . . On Thursday my mind was deeply exer-
cised on the subject of sanctification; and the result was, a determination to preach it more frequently, and pursue it more diligently."

Frequently he speaks of preaching upon this
theme, and of those who testify to having received
it. On Thursday, Feb. 21, 1782, he says; "I am
filled with love from day to day. O, bless the Lord
for the constant communion I enjoy with him!
Sanctification is the doctrine which is most wanted
to be preached among the people here, whom the
more I know the more I love; Antinomians are
laboring to spread their tenets among them; but
they will give way, as holiness of heart and life is
pointedly enforced and pressed home upon their

consciences. This is the best antidote to the poison." Vol. 1, p. 441.

August 6, 1786, he writes, "A pleasing thought passed through my mind: it was this, *that I was saved from the remains of sin.* As yet, I have felt no returns thereof." Vol. 1, p. 516.

Again, on page 137 of Vol. 2, he says; "For months past I have felt as if in the possession of perfect love; not a moment's desire of anything but God." 1791.

On page 152 of same volume he breaks out in a rapture of praise; "I would not live always; hail! happy death; nothing but holiness, perfect love, and then glory for me!" 1792.

In speaking of a certain place, he says: "I feel the death of the district. I see what is wanting here—discipline, *and the preaching a present and full salvation, and the enforcement of the doctrine of sanctification.*"

From this it seems that he, like Wesley, believed that the preaching of the doctrine always caused the work of God to prosper.

In Vol. III. p 105, he says: "I find the way of *holiness* very narrow to walk in or to preach; and although I do not consider *sanctification—Chris-*

tian perfection, commonplace subjects, *yet I make them the burden, and labor to make them the savour of every sermon."*   Mar. 7, 1803.

Again, on page 237 of same volume, he says, "I feel as if I ought not to preach one sermon without being pointed and very full upon *the doctrine of purity."*   Oct. 1, 1806.

Again he takes the witness stand. 'My body is very feeble, but my soul enjoys *perfect love* and *perfect peace."*   p 316, 1809.

"I live in patience, in purity, and in the perfect love of God."   p 432, 1814.

"Dust, fever, and too much company, these are my trials; peace, and perfect love, these are my consolations." p 450, 1815.

"I live in God from moment to moment." p 471, Dec. 2, 1815.

This is next to the last entry in his journal. On March 21, 1816, he passed in triumph to his eternal reward.

We have now given the testimony of the leaders in British and American Methodism, and will now turn to some of the lesser, but equally reliable witnesses.

William Carvasso was born in England on Mar.

11, 1750. He became one of the greatest, if not *the* greatest, class-leader Methodism has produced. His memoir is published by our Book Concern. We will insert some extracts from it.

"The very moment I formed this resolution (to never cease crying for mercy) in my heart, Christ appeared within, and God pardoned all my sins, and set my soul at liberty. The Spirit itself now bore witness with my spirit that I was a child of God. This was about nine o'clock, May 6, 1771; and never shall I forget that happy hour." p 33.

"In the same happy frame of mind * * * * *I went on for the space of three months not expecting any more conflicts; but, O, how greatly I was mistaken! * * * *I was soon taught * * * * that I had not only to contend with Satan and the world from without, but with inward enemies also; which now began to make no small stir. * * * * My inward nature appeared so black and sinful, that I felt it impossible to rest in that state. *Some, perhaps, will imagine that this may have arisen from the want of knowledge of forgiveness. That could not be the case, for I never had one doubt of my acceptance; the witness was so clear, that Satan himself knew it was in vain to attack me from* *that quarter.* * * * *What I now wanted was "inward holiness," and for this I prayed and searched the Scriptures, * * * *. Many were the hard struggles which I had with unbelief, and Satan told me that if I ever should get it, I should never be able to retain it. * * * * * At length, one evening, while engaged in a prayer meeting, the great deliverance came. I began to exercise faith, by believing. 'I shall have the blessing now.' * * * no sooner had I uttered or spoken the words from my heart, * * * * than refining fire went through my heart,—illuminated my soul. * * * * I then *received the full witness of the Spirit that the blood of Jesus had cleansed me from all sin.* * * * This happy change took place in my soul Mar. 13, 1772." pp. 33-38.

No comment is needed. While still enjoying acceptance with God, he felt his need of, sought and found the "Second Blessing." He was a class-leader for over fifty years, and was an instrument in the hands of God in the conversion and sanctification of hundreds of souls.

Bishop Whatcoat, and Bishop Hamline, were also witnesses to this full salvation.

Dr. Stephen Olin, once President of Wesleyan

University, and possessed of one of the profound-
est minds of his age, said: "I sometimes say to
my intimate friends that I have great comfort in
believing *that I have been made a partaker of thi*
grace." At another time before many visitors and
friends of the college alumni and students, he
arose in a general class-meeting and said he "desired to make known the fact that he experienced,
and was conscious of enjoying daily and hourly,
the blessing of *perfect love."*

Bishop R. S. Foster, a profound theologian, who
had one of the finest and most cultivated minds
in the church speaks thus of his experience: "Here
again the Spirit seemed to lead me into the inmost sanctuary of my soul,—into those cham-
bers where I had before discovered such defilement,
and showed me that all was cleansed, that the cor-
ruptions which had given me such distress were
dead—taken away, that not one of them remained.
I felt the truth of the witness; it was so; I was
conscious of it, *as conscious as I ever had been of*
my conversion." Guide to Holiness, 1850.

Charles G. Finney, once President of Oberlin
College, and one of the great evangelists of the
centuries, owes his success to the baptism of the

Spirit received as a conscious experience *after* he had already had a marvelous manifestation of Christ to his soul. He says, "1 could feel the impression like a wave of electricity going through and through me. Indeed, it seemed to come in waves and waves of liquid love. It seemed like the very breath of God. No words can express the wonderful love that was shed abroad in my heart. I wept aloud with joy and love; and I do not know but I should say I literally bellowed out the unutterable gushings of my heart.

"These waves came over me and over me and over me, until I cried out; 'I shall die if these waves continue to pass over me. Lord, I can not bear any more!"

We will give one more witness to the second blessing, and then rest our case with the confidence that it is established as certainly as any matter of fact can be established by means of witnesses.

D. L. Moody, a short time bfore his death while preaching in Brooklyn, made this statement: "I know that if I should be asked to be a witness in court, my testimony would be taken; and I want you to take my testimony as to what it is to be filled with the Spirit. There are *two* epochs in my

life which stand out clear. One is, when I was between eighteen and nineteen years old, when I was
born of the Spirit. There never can come a greater blessing to a man on this earth than to be born
again—born from above;—to have the God nature
planted in him. God has been good to me. He
has showered blessing after blessing upon me; *but
the greatest blessing,* next to being born again,
came *sixteen years after, when I was filled with
the Spirit,* and it has never left me."

These witnesses might be greatly multiplied
from the various denominations, but this would
not materially increase the certainty of the matter. Two or three competent and impartial witnesses are sufficient to establish any matter of fact.

We might give the testimony of some who
once opposed the teaching with all their might,
but afterwards, like Saul of Tarsus, received the
blessing and became the champion of the "Way"
they once persecuted; but we desist,

Our case is won. To deny the testimony of these
men to the *"second blessing"* is also to call in question the validity of their testimony to regeneration,
and who is ready for such an undertaking? To

succeed would be to undermine the very foundations of Christianity.

In conclusion let us say, we believe there is no room left for dispute as to the *"second blesing"* doctrine being Methodistic.

The success of Methodism in the world in overcoming all opposing forces, and in tranforming the character and the very nature of the men and women who accepted its teaching, *in only• paralleled by primitive Christianity.* Two factors enter into this success, (1.) their doctrine, (2.) their discipline. *But without the possession of the experience as set forth in the doctrine, their discipline would be an impossibility.* So we infer that the secrets of their succcs lies in the doctrine of a full and complete salvation from all sin.

It seems to us that no other explanation is possible.

This doctrine preached, possessed, and lived, is to Methodism what Samson's locks were to him.

Has "Delilah" taken Methodism by her wiles and is she now, "grinding for the Philistines?"

We draw the curtain over the scene . Let each Methodist, high and low, on his knees before God, answer for himself.

"And may the very God of peace himself, sanctify you *wholly*; and may your spirit and soul, and
body be preserved entire, without blame at the
coming of our Lord Jesus Christ. Faithful is he
that calleth you, who also will do it." I Thess. 5:
23, 24.

The end.

www.ingramcontent.com/pod-product-compliance
Lightning Source LLC
Chambersburg PA
CBHW020040040426
42331CB00030B/114